Missionaries
Miners
and Indians

To Stuart Voss, I from whom am always learning, Evelyn Hu-DeHart St Louis June 1982

The Sonora and Sinaloa Missions, by Father Jose Palomino, 1744

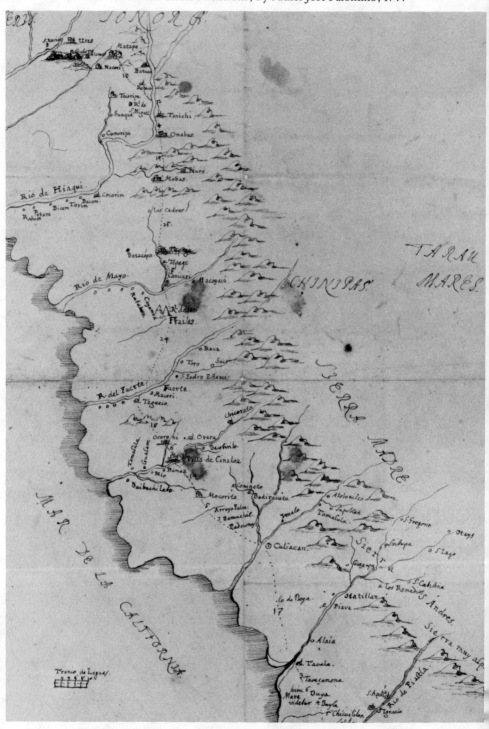

From: Ernest J. Burrus, *Obra cartográfica de la Provincia de México de la Compañia de Jesús* (Madrid: J. Porrua Turanzas, 1967), map no. 43.

Missionaries
Miners
and Indians

*Spanish Contact with the Yaqui Nation
of Northwestern New Spain
1533 – 1820*

Evelyn Hu-DeHart

THE UNIVERSITY OF ARIZONA PRESS
Tucson, Arizona

About the author...

Evelyn Hu-DeHart's volume on the colonial experience of the Yaqui people was
the first of a series covering the course of Yaqui history into the twentieth
century. In 1972, she was awarded a Foreign Area Fellowship to do research in
Mexico on the history of the Yaqui people of Sonora. In 1974, she began teaching
Latin American history at Washington University in St. Louis. Professor
Hu-DeHart received a Ph.D. in Latin American History in 1976 from the Uni-
versity of Texas at Austin. She has a B.A. in Political Science from Stanford
University, and she has studied in Brazil with a Fulbright Scholarship and in
Spain. Born in Chungking, China, Professor Hu-DeHart immigrated with her
family to the United States in 1959.

THE UNIVERSITY OF ARIZONA PRESS

This book was set in 10/12 Bembo on a V.I.P.

Copyright 1981
The Arizona Board of Regents
All Rights Reserved
Manufactured in the U.S.A.

Library of Congress Cataloging in Publication Data

Hu-DeHart, Evelyn.
    Missionaries, miners, and Indians.

    Bibliography: p.
    Includes index.
    1. Yaqui Indians — Missions.   2. Jesuits — Missions
— Mexico.   3. Yaqui Indians — Government relations.
4. Indians of Mexico — Missions.   5. Indians of
Mexico — Government relations.   6. Yaqui Indians —
Wars, 1740.   I. Title.
F1221.Y3H82   972'.00497   81-14658

ISBN 0-8165-0740-6   AACR2
ISBN 0-8165-0755-4 (pbk.)

To my mother and father
who taught me to survive

To the Yaqui people
who fight to survive
and can teach us all

Contents

viii   *Contents*

Tables

Maps

CHAPTER 1

The Colonial Legacy

In the last decades of the twentieth century, the Yaqui Indians were among the few remnant indigenous nations of the vast region comprising northwestern Mexico and the southwestern United States. Four centuries of contact and warfare with the *yori* or white man had not forcefully assimilated or decimated a proud people bent on survival. Thirty thousand strong at the time of Spanish conquest in the early sixteenth century, an estimated 15,000 still existed, the bulk of them in the vicinity of the Yaqui River, their traditional homeland in southern Sonora, Mexico. A few thousand were scattered throughout Mexico, western, and particularly southwestern United States, some clustering around their own communities-in-exile such as those just outside Tucson, Arizona, sixty miles north of the border and the Mexican state of Sonora.

Since the Mexican Revolution of 1910, despite the rhetoric of social justice and agrarian reform, Yaquis had not exercised much control over the land and its resources. To be sure, in the late 1930s progressive

President Lázaro Cárdenas created a *zona indígena* — a de facto reservation — on the north bank of the Yaqui River to provide the Yaqui people with some land and territorial integrity. However, the Indians did not enjoy the concurrent guarantee of water, which is absolutely indispensable for making the rich soil produce at capacity. With few exceptions, those Yaquis who remained on the land were limited to subsistence agriculture, their poverty all the more sharpened in contrast to the prosperous commercial agriculture which large Mexican farmers practiced on the south side of the river. There, an abundance of water from government-built dams, capital from private and public sources, and technology derived partly from the Green Revolution* have developed the Yaqui River Valley into a well-known showcase of Mexico's postwar "economic miracle." In sum, it seemed ironic that, while alone among Mexico's Indian peasantry the Yaquis possessed rich land, they were not significantly better off.

In addition to the paradox in the late twentieth century, or perhaps because of it, most Yaquis proudly claim a separate ethnic and cultural identity, the hallmark of their character being to regard themselves first and foremost as "the Yaqui people" — distinct from the Mexican cultural mainstream or from any social class in the larger social structure. This definite self-image has prevailed through the entire course of a long and often violent history of contact with yoris.

Of course, Indian resistance to acculturation and assimilation is not uncommon in Mexican history. The Yaquis stand out for having waged the most determined, enduring, and successful war against involuntary absorption into the dominant culture or integration with the larger society. In response to persistent outside pressures to transform themselves irreversibly and on alien terms, they have held on tenaciously to their land, community, and culture, guarantees of their autonomy. Even as they are losing the battle in the course of the twentieth century, they have not yet surrendered the ethos of resistance. In the words

---

*Ironically, the Rockefeller-financed Green Revolution, conceived to produce enough staple grains to feed the world's hungry masses, had served only to widen the gap between rich and poor, between subsistence and capitalist, commercial agriculture. In both Mexico and India, where the grain experiments took place, the actual beneficiaries of the new technology were the large private landowners, who alone could afford the heavy investment in farm machinery, fertilizer, and insecticide necessary for the cultivation of the new hybrid strains. For a general critique, *see:* Harry M. Cleaver, "The Contradictions of the Green Revolution," *Monthly Review* 24 (1972), pp. 80–111; for a specific discussion of the Mexican case, *see:* Cynthia Hewitt de Alcántara, *Modernizing Mexican Agriculture: Socioeconomic Implications of Technological Change 1940–1970* (Geneva: United Nations Research Institute for Social Development, 1976).

of a Yaqui laborer, recorded in the 1960s, "There will always be a Yaqui tribe. The Yaquis are not like the Mayos or the Pimas, who have all become Mexicans."*

The Influence of the Jesuits

Significantly, the Yaquis' own historical memory in the twentieth century dated back to the period of Jesuit reorganization, but not earlier. And it was this legacy that Yaquis sought to preserve by themselves well into the nineteenth and twentieth centuries. The profound impact of the long, intense Jesuit missionary experience must be judged decisive in explaining the survival of the Yaqui people as a culturally intact and politically autonomous people at the end of the colonial period. Jesuits never intended their directed cultural change to prepare Yaquis for assimilation into the larger, exploitative Spanish social structure. Rather, in reorganizing Yaqui society and economy, in protecting Yaquis against Spanish encroachment on their land and restraining indiscriminate uses of their labor, and in fighting a protracted war against secularization, Jesuits hoped to safeguard the Yaquis' welfare and, in so doing, their own institutional interests as well. For only when the indigenous peoples remained healthy and intact could the missions endure. Moreover, a productive mission economy guaranteed expansion of the Jesuit evangelical empire. To the Yaquis, the tightly organized mission system gave them a more precise definition of their territorial boundaries, a stronger sense of cultural unity, and a greater degree of economic security. The imposed experience compressed in time social developments that would have taken much longer in a more natural evolution. In short, the mission accelerated in all Yaqui speakers the sense of being one people, or, in the Jesuits' preferred term, one nation.

From the beginning, Jesuits confronted a paradox which they themselves had helped create. Like all institutions, the Jesuit empire sought to perpetuate itself. In order to keep the Indians in a permanent state of dependency, they took charge of every aspect of Yaqui life, going far beyond the original purpose of doctrinal education and conversion. Initial tutelage and guidance soon became institutionalized into a system of paternalistic, autocratic rule. In assuming ultimate political authority,

---

*Rosalío Moisés, Jane Holden Kelly, and William Curry Holden, *The Tall Candle: The Personal Chronicle of a Yaqui Indian* (Lincoln: University of Nebraska Press, 1971), p. 239. It is interesting that with noticeable disdain Moisés picked out Mayos and Pimas to compare with Yaquis. Until the late nineteenth century, Pimas and especially Mayos had also fiercely resisted integration with Mexican society and frequently fought alongside Yaquis against Mexican troops. In the 1960s, although they still retained a sense of their Indian identities, they were rapidly being absorbed into the dominant society.

missionaries undercut the power of local Yaqui magistrates who were nominally the Crown's representatives. The fathers discouraged all Yaqui initiative and leadership to the point of preferring to promote outsiders as administrative assistants in the Yaqui mission. Under the Jesuit system, for more than 100 years all Yaquis appeared to be one docile collective, without an independent leader or spokesman. In managing communal economic activities and administering the disposal of the enormous surpluses Yaquis produced, missionaries preempted the role of a native ruling class which normally would have appeared with the rise of a surplus economy. Thus when Jesuits were expelled in 1767 Yaqui society remained essentially a nonhierarchical, classless community and, with the departure of the Jesuit managers and their rationale for large-scale production, reverted to subsistence farming, harvesting only a small excess to support the new resident priests and keep up the village churches.

The Influence of Spanish Secular Society

The Jesuits' absolutist control and the mission's geographical and social insulation, however, did not prevent some Yaquis from periodically escaping the tight system. As early as the second half of the seventeenth century, a trickle of mostly young males ventured to leave their pueblos for temporary work in established northern mines. Few ever deserted the mission permanently, however, most returning after a brief sojourn. Their situation was unlike that of many Indians from sedentary, densely settled central New Spain who also drifted to the northern *reales de minas,* or mining centers, around the same time. Faced with the disintegration of their communities caused by drastic depopulation and widespread loss of land and waters to Spanish colonists, these Indians had no choice but to seek a new livelihood. They had little prospect of returning home, only the grim destiny of fading into the nebulous culture of the growing mestizo masses around the camps. Thanks largely to the missionaries, Yaquis were never subject to this harsh fate, but retained a stable and secure home community. For them the mines presented an occasional diversion from the more regimented routine of mission life and an outside source of income that allowed them to purchase and enjoy certain goods not otherwise available to them.

Of course, the missionaries never sanctioned the Yaquis' mobility. However, their adamant opposition met with equally persistent challenge from the miners and *hacendados,* or Spanish landowners, of a struggling secular society whose promises for development depended critically on free access to the mission populations for labor. New mines discovered in Sonora, Ostimuri, and Sinaloa near the end of the seventeenth century intensified Spanish interest in that region and seriously threatened Jesuit hegemony. But mounting pressures on the Jesuits to compromise only made them more resistant to change and led them to view the 1740 Yaqui rebellion as the result of a conspiracy to promote secularization, blinding them to any possible distinction between internal tensions and outside demands.

The precipitant of the one and only major Yaqui uprising was floods and ensuing famine, aggravated by the resident fathers' insensitive handling of the food crisis. The real issues went deeper than hunger. As articulated by the first Yaqui leadership that arose independently of the Jesuits, after a century of tutelage the time had come to revise certain fundamental practices in the mission. Essentially, the Yaquis wanted their missionaries to reduce the excessive demands on their labor and to loosen their paternalistic, authoritarian rule, so that the people could exercise greater control over their own lives. Although it seemed unlikely that the Yaqui leaders acted as mere pawns for Spanish interests, nevertheless some of their demands coincided with secular designs to weaken the mission system. To their ultimate detriment, Jesuits reacted solely to a perceived Spanish conspiracy. In denying any legitimacy to the Yaquis' grievances, they in effect encouraged the Indians to circumvent the system rather than to work within it. When the reform-minded Bourbon monarchy finally expelled the monopolistic Jesuits in 1767, the act intensified an ongoing erosion of Jesuit power in the northwest that had begun with their myopic understanding and strong reactions to the 1740 crisis.

After the rebellion, more and more Yaquis took to the mines. Although Jesuits never relented in principle, their markedly subdued spirits betrayed a resignation to the inevitable migration. But as before, few of the mobile Yaquis stayed away permanently. Nor were any forced to remain in the mining camps beyond their will, for the competition for manpower in the labor-scarce northern frontier militated against the growth of debt peonage—already prevalent as a device to tie down necessary workers in the central and southern parts of the viceroyalty. Moreover, by mid-eighteenth century, Yaquis had an urgent reason to protect their homes and villages: for the first time in their history, Yaquis felt the need to defend their mission community against marauding Indians. Working closely with local military authorities in this new activity also reinforced their independence from the missionaries, who in turn lost their monopoly on authority. Furthermore, the defense function consolidated a military tradition for the Yaquis, embodied in the newly institutionalized militia and captain-general position. Largely on their own initiative, Yaquis managed to balance the two priorities: providing labor for the mines and protecting their pueblos.

The migration also represented the Yaquis' own way of responding to pressures of the expanding secular society around them, demonstrating a flexibility that contrasted sharply with the Jesuits' intransigence. Viewing any change in the mission system as a serious threat to their presence, in the end the fathers' uncompromising attitude lost them their entire mission system. Yaquis, on the other hand, were able to salvage much of their community and culture. After the 1767 Jesuit expulsion, Yaquis sensed more than ever that if they supplied the thriving mining economy with adequate labor, then they might expect less official interference in how they lived their own lives in their own villages. When José de Gálvez attempted to implement land reforms in the Yaqui River and simultaneously stimulate mining production, Yaquis were the first to perceive and then to take advantage of a basic conflict between these two goals. While the land reforms were part of a long-range plan to integrate Yaquis and other long-missionized Indians as tax-paying peasants into the larger social system and eventually to gain access to their surplus land, the mines required an immediate and steady supply of dependable, experienced workers, which to a large extent meant Yaquis. Both purposes rested on the acquiescence and massive participation of the Indian people. When Yaquis practiced their particular type of rotational migration between mission and mine, they created a demographic instability in the pueblos which rendered impossible any permanent division and assignment of land or the collection of taxes at regular intervals. At the same time, by making themselves an indispensable part of the mining economy, they discouraged pressures on them to submit to reforms that might reduce their mobility.

Nor did the rotational migration seriously weaken the Yaqui's ability or erode their commitment to preserve that culture and autonomy which constituted their legacy from the Jesuits. In this endeavor, they received valuable help and support from the new secular priests. Although occasionally Yaquis felt the need to assert their political independence, it did not appear that Spaniards jeopardized their life style in any fundamental way during the closing period of the colony. At that time, the Crown and *vecinos,* or Spanish residents, in the northwest clearly coveted Yaqui labor more than their land, produce, or taxes. Also, the Yaquis' geographical position — protected by mountains and the sea on three sides, bounded by the Mayos to the south — might have shielded them from more intense Spanish encroachment. In addition, during the colonial period no significant mines were discovered or exploited inside Yaqui territory, although several famous ones were not far away.*

When nineteenth-century Mexicans and foreigners began to value Yaqui land as much as Yaqui labor, the Yaquis' unique compromise with the larger environment came to a violent end. After Mexico's independence from Spain in 1826, this industrious and basically pacific people who had rebelled only once during the long Jesuit and Bourbon periods waged an almost unceasing war with the white man against loss of land, culture, and autonomy.

---

*Even though there are still no famous mines located within Yaqui territory, a persistent belief among Sonorans, Mexicans in general, and foreigners in the nineteenth and twentieth centuries was that the area was enormously rich in precious minerals. Yet the bitter yoris contend that Yaquis have stubbornly kept outsiders from exploiting such minerals, while refusing to mine any themselves. The legend has become the source of many stories, including the work of noted Texas writer J. Frank Dobie, entitled *Apache Gold and Yaqui Silver* (see Bibliography).

CHAPTER 2

Before the Jesuits

The modern Mexican states of Sonora, Chihuahua, and northern Sinaloa, as well as parts of the North American states of Arizona and New Mexico, make up what used to be the nebulous northwestern frontier of New Spain. The northern border was eventually stabilized at the Gila River in Arizona. Sonora and Sinaloa, considered one political unit until the nineteenth century, are separated from Chihuahua by the Sierra Madre Occidental and bordered on the west by the Gulf of California. During the Spanish colonial era, this entire northern territory was first known as the kingdom *(reino)* of Nueva Vizcaya and later as the Internal Provinces.

Inhabited for many thousand years before the arrival of Spaniards in the early sixteenth century, northwestern New Spain contained over 100 different indigenous nations, with an estimated aboriginal population of 540,000. The area is basically arid and desertlike, with pockets of more hospitable, semiarid environments located in the rugged Sierra Madre and along a series of rivers that cut through the Sierra to the Gulf.[1] For most of the peoples, a life of hunting and gathering was giving way to a more sedentary, horticultural existence. None of them, however, was even approaching the advanced civilizations of central and southern Mexico, although there were definite links in language and agriculture. Anthropologists have concluded that farming techniques and crops were transmitted northward from group to group. The six major languages of the northwest and Nahuatl spoken by the Mexican people of the center all belong to the Uto-Aztecan linguistic stock.[2]

Ethnographers and geographers have divided the northern peoples into several major groupings according to location, cultural level, and language. Their Spanish-given, rather than the original, indigenous names, are the ones that have survived in the historical records. Those grouped as *barranca* peoples once dwelled in the deep canyons and warm valley lands of the Sierra Madre summits, in the present Mexican states of Sonora, Sinaloa, and Chihuahua. Numerically small, culturally divergent, and linguistically undetermined, Acaxees, Xiximees, and other barranca peoples had become extinct long ago. Along the coast, from the Culiacán to the Altar rivers, small bands of nonagriculturalists lived in desert enclaves. Most hardy and well known of these seminomadic peoples are the Seris of Sonora, some 200 of whom still exist under extremely miserable conditions. The plateau margins of Chihuahua, New Mexico, and Arizona harbored the legendary Athapaskans, seminomads who cultivated beans and maize when they could. For over three centuries, Apaches, Navajos, and other Athapaskans terrorized the frontiers of New Spain, Mexico, and the United States. In the twentieth century, their greatly reduced number of survivors live mainly in American reservations. Papagos of Sonora and the American Southwest are also survivors. They have an agricultural heritage, but their desert habitat has made permanent settlements difficult.[3]

By far the largest and densest, the most agricultural and sedentary, were the *ranchería* peoples of the northwest, so named by anthropologist Edward Spicer after the type of communities they built. Rancherías were sprawling, loosely organized collections of huts, which were normally uncontiguous and ranged in number from several tens to several hundreds. These communities were not permanently located, since they shifted according to availability of arable land.

Pimas and Opatas are two surviving ranchería peoples. At one time Pimas were widely distributed over what is now southwestern United States – northwestern Mexico, their territory embracing a variety of environments and climates. Pima rancherías, though more compact than others, still did not approach the organization of permanent villages. Nor did a shared common language among all Pimas lead to their integration as one unified political and social unit. Located in a more restricted corner of Sonora, Opata rancherías formed another loosely federated group which shared a common language but did not obey any central political authority. Most Pimas and Opatas lived in inland river basins and valleys.[4]

Located along the major waterways of the Gulf of California coast, Cáhitaspeakers were the most populous and culturally most advanced ranchería peoples. The Sinaloa, Fuerte, Mayo, and Yaqui rivers all originate in the Sierra Madre, snaking westward until they pour into the Gulf, their rich alluvial plains and valleys forming the fertile agricultural lands which could support dense populations. The Suaqui (or Fuerteño), Mayo, Yaqui, Ocoroni, Ahome, Tehueco, Cinaloa, Conicari, Macoyahui, and Tepahue peoples all spoke mutually intelligible Cáhita tongues. Yaquis and their close neighbors, the Mayos, are the only surviving members of this large group.

The Yaqui River is the longest, most copious, and most important waterway of the Mexican northwest. It springs from high in the Sierra Madre and winds southwestward for over 400 miles before disgorging into the Gulf, at a point near the present port of Guaymas, Sonora. Occupying the rich alluvial plains of its lower course were the Yaquis, the largest group of Cáhita-speaking people. Early missionaries estimated a total aboriginal population of 30,000, distributed among eighty rancherías. Most of them were dispersed on both sides of the river, covering an area about sixty miles long and fifteen miles wide.[5] The average ranchería size would have been about 400 persons, although actual sizes varied greatly. The bilateral extended family, or maternal and paternal kinship lines, constituted the basic social and economic unit, with several such families probably forming a ranchería. Since marriage was exogamous, some kind of kinship ties existed between rancherías. A density of approximately thirty persons per square mile made the Yaqui territory the most densely populated area in the whole northwest.[6]

Yaquis had access to the resources of a region much larger than the margins of the river itself. Stretching from the Gulf of California to the Sierra Madre range, for a total surface of about 3,500 square miles, this territory can be divided into three zones. The area at the mouth of the river is basically arid, characterized by desert vegetation. Rancherías located in this part depended heavily on the foods of the sea for sustenance. The middle section of "extensive valleys and splendid canyons bathed by the Yaqui" is the lush, fertile zone that has given the Yaqui its eternal fame. Most of the rancherías were concentrated here and engaged primarily in agriculture, with dwellings built near the cultivated fields. Flanking this section on the north is an elongated mountain range called the Sierra de Bacatete, forming a mountainous third section. Missionaries called the small number of hunters and gatherers in this zone *monteraces,* or mountain people.[7]

Most Yaquis were agriculturists, planting maize as the major crop, but also beans, squash, gourds, tobacco, cotton, and other seeds. They did not depend entirely on direct precipitation to cultivate their fields and planted two or even three harvests a year. They could usually count on the river receiving sufficient rainfall from the mountains east of their territory to innundate the lowland delta, making possible spring crops on fields not directly irrigated by precipitation. At the same time, since the Yaquis did not practice controlled irrigation, excessive flooding appeared to have been their most serious natural disaster.

Their primitive farming methods and simple techniques were embodied in one implement—the digging stick, which seemed sufficient for their needs. With the warm climate, a harvest was possible within three months after spring planting, usually before the advent of summer rains in July.[8] A smaller crop could be planted in the winter, although this was not always done. Specific information on aboriginal planting and harvesting rites is lacking. With a yield as high as 100 to 1 under optimal conditions, all indications suggest that the Yaquis lived in a world of plenty.

Land ownership was communal, while usufruct was family based. With enough irrigated land for every household, usage rights could have been established through assignment by the ranchería or by the individual household head staking out a claim on his own. Each family was a self-reliant economic unit with everyone—men, women, and children— active in production. There is no evidence of labor exploitation of one group by another, of division of labor by household or ranchería, or of collective economic activity on any regular basis. Living from harvest to harvest, husbanding no food, and producing no surplus, Yaquis resorted to hunting and gathering when food ran out or when floods struck. It is possible that under the most severe food crises, the entire ranchería might have come together and assumed collective responsibility to weather the hardships.[9]

Ranchería houses were temporary structures, usually made of mats *(petatlán)* and canes *(carrizo)* and occasionally of mud. Women did some simple weaving, using native-grown cotton, as well as some utilitarian basketry and pottery work. Bows and arrows, sometimes poisoned, were the major weapons. Tobacco was grown for use in certain rituals and in curing.[10]

Being essentially self-sufficient, Yaquis engaged in trade only in a limited and sporadic way; women exchanged coastal salt and fish for inland crops and luxury items, such as multicolored feathers much coveted for personal ornamentation.[11] This simple trade also served the Yaquis as a system of communication and intelligence gathering.

Information on aboriginal religious and political organizations is scanty and incomplete. Just as each ranchería was an autonomous unit economically, so it appeared to be a politically self-contained entity during peacetime. While each ranchería had several elders or spokesmen, no one individual exercised a centralized authority or enjoyed sufficiently widespread prestige to direct the affairs of all the rancherías during normal times. In some form of open council, each community deliberated and decided on its own matters.

The system of leadership changed, however, during times of crisis, such as wars. When Yaquis perceived a direct, external threat to all of them, they swiftly banded together to mobilize a fighting force consisting of all adult males, estimated to have been as high as 8,000 to 10,000. An ad hoc committee of warriors and elders from all rancherías convened to act as a war council. Military leaders, distinguishing themselves by dress and manner, emerged to take charge on the battlefield. Yaquis accorded these designated chiefs absolute obedience during the emergency. Wars appeared to have been the only occasions when all rancherías consistently united for a common purpose and for the common good.[12] Nevertheless, this limited and conditional unity already set the Yaquis apart as more cohesive than any other people in the northwest.

Proven military leaders then seemed to retain some of their earned prestige during peacetime, graduating with time into the status of ranchería elders. When the first Spaniards and missionaries arrived, because of their own European culture and previous experience with more advanced civilizations of Mesoamerica, they always tried to identify the chiefs, whom they called *caciques* or *principales*. Since their initial encounters with Yaquis usually provoked hostile reactions, chiefs or leaders readily appeared. On the other hand, when they were no longer at war with Yaquis, to their puzzlement they found that those men whom they had thought to be chiefs wielded in fact rather limited power, their authority restricted within ranchería boundaries.

A dearth of information on Yaqui religion and ceremonies has yielded only a superficial appreciation of this important aspect of aboriginal culture. Spanish explorers were not notably interested in Yaqui religious life, especially since there were no overt structures and few symbols, rituals, or personnel to command their attention, contrary again to their experience in central and southern Mexico. The few ceremonies Spaniards did observe and record were ritual hunts and peace celebrations, events which all resulted from the early violent confrontations.[13]

Indeed, Jesuits noticed the lack of idols, ceremonial centers, and communal religious cults. But since Yaquis erected no permanent or fixed ritual sites, such as temples, and destroyed whatever symbols of worship they used immediately after the ceremonies, much of the aboriginal practices undoubtedly eluded the zealous attention of the first missionaries. Nevertheless, even as they hastened to extirpate what little they found, the early fathers tried to retain and incorporate some indigenous music and dances into the new Christian festivals they introduced.[14]

Aboriginal Yaqui religion can best be described as totemic. The essence of totemism is a close, direct relationship between the individual and supernatural "guardian spirits," manifested in the forms of plants, animals, and even other human beings. In this system, there was no organized, professional priesthood. Persons especially gifted at inducing the supernatural, or unusually guided by the spirits, were known as *hechiceros* (Spanish term used by the first Jesuits; original Yaqui term not noted), shamans or medicine men. Besides being ritual specialists, supervising the various ceremonies, they also acted as diagnosticians and medicine men. Through dreams and trances, they determined the causes of illnesses and prescribed the cures. A particularly skilled hechicero shared with the bravest warriors the high esteem of his community.[15] As with other respected individuals, hechiceros were not full-time specialists, did not inherit their positions although they might have their skills, and did not constitute a distinct, privileged hierarchy in Yaqui society. To retain his prestige, an hechicero had to prove his magical and healing prowesses constantly. Summarizing Yaqui totemic religion, Mexican scholar Miguel Othón de Mendizábal observed: "The absence of a collective cult, of an organized and hierarchical priesthood, consequently led each individual to be the priest of his own cult, the interpreter of his own religion, and the judge of his own conduct."[16] To have control over one's life, to assume responsibility for one's actions, are legacies of the surviving Yaqui people from this distant pre-Hispanic past.

The fundamental or primitive egalitarian and democratic nature of aboriginal Yaqui society was associated with a low material culture. Before the production of economic surpluses, society had no need for, and no means to support, elites or specialists removed from the direct act of production. Without a social hierarchy or a ruling class, there was consequently no state, nor were there population centers remotely resembling towns and cities.

Spanish arrival in the early sixteenth century coincided with a period of demographic expansion to the northwest. The increasingly frequent boundary wars with neighbors began to develop in the Yaquis a sense of territoriality that embraced all their rancherías. This emerging attitude conditioned the early Yaqui responses to the first Spanish intrusions.

First Spanish Intrusions

Soon after his conquest of the Aztec empire in central Mexico, Hernán Crotés turned his curious and avaricious eyes to the unknown regions of the north. Among his many rivals for new fame and glory was the notorious Nuño Beltrán de Guzmán, noted for his terroristic raids for Indian slaves. Stirring rumors of legendary, fabulously rich kingdoms far to the north—the Seven Cities of Cíbola, the kingdom of the Gran Quivara, and the Kingdom of the Amazons—fed the uncontainable fantasies of Cortés, Guzmán, and other compatriots. For Cortés, his several ambitious projects in 1532 to 1536 to explore the northwestern coast and the Gulf of California (Sea of Cortés) were not to match his glorious earlier achievements.[17] Guzmán's land explorations brought somewhat better results.

In 1529, with 500 Spaniards and thousands of impressed Indian auxiliaries, Guzmán undertook the first of a series of explorations into the northwest. He pushed well beyond the Cañas River, the southern boundary of the modern Mexican state of Sinaloa, covering a territory that came to be known as the provinces of Chiametla, Piaxtla, and Culiacán during the colonial period. Some of his men went as far north as the Sinaloa (Petatlán) River. Guzmán failed to locate anything resembling the cities of Cíbola, but he founded San Miguel on the Culiacán, the first Spanish settlement in the northwest, and granted each of the Spaniards who stayed behind an *encomienda,* or quota, of tributary Indians. For his troubles, the Crown made Guzmán first governor of the new kingdom of Nueva Galicia in 1531.[18]

Although as governor Guzmán gave up active exploration himself, his interest in the northwest did not abate. The 1533 expedition he dispatched under the command of Captain Diego de Guzmán penetrated farther north than ever before, into the upper limits of the Cáhita-speaking peoples, and brought back news of the Yaquis for the first time. An Anonymous Reporter, a member of the party, kept a close diary of this momentous journey.

Leaving Culiacán in July, the Spaniards reached the Mayo River by September, having crossed the Sinaloa and Fuerte (Zuaque or Suaque) rivers a month earlier.[19] The Mayo people's initial hostility towards the uninvited guests mellowed considerably when the Spaniards indicated they would not tarry long. So eager were the Mayos to be rid of the strangers that they supplied the travelers with dried corn, salt, and even a guide.

On 4 October 1533, the expedition arrived at the Yaqui River, or, as the Anonymous Reporter spelled it, the Yaquimí.* Captain Guzmán performed the customary first act of all Spanish *conquistadores* in claiming the river and all its inhabitants for the King of Spain. He then officially renamed it in Spanish the San Francisco River, a name which never took hold.[20] Shortly afterwards, the first encounter between Spaniards and Yaquis occurred. In the words of the Anonymous Reporter, as the exploration party marched downstream

> those who went ahead returned to tell us that there were warriors waiting for us ahead. So we gathered our things and, dividing ourselves into a vanguard and a rearguard, marched towards the Indian warriors, who were assembled in a large field of one-and-a-half leagues. When they saw us, they began to march towards us very boldly, throwing fistfuls of dirt into the air, flexing their bows and making fierce grimaces.

The intruders had no difficulty picking out the leader of this formidable adversary. According to the Anonymous Reporter he was

> an old man more distinguished than the others, because he wore a black robe like a scapulary, studded with pearls, and surrounded by dogs, birds and deer and many other things. And as it was morning, and the sunlight fell on him, he blazed like silver. He carried his bow and arrows, and a wooden staff with a very elaborate handle, and was in control of the people.

Further impressing the Spaniards, the old man drew a line on the ground as a demarcation, threatening death to any intruder who dared cross it. Then, to Captain Guzmán's protestations of peaceful intentions and request for food, the Yaquis replied that they would gladly oblige if the Spaniards would allow themselves and their horses to be tied up. Whereupon the Spaniards decided the time had come for them to seize the initiative and attack. "So aiming our heaviest canon at them, we shouted 'Santiago' as we fired it, and pounded on them."

While chauvinistically claiming a Spanish victory even as they retreated, the Anonymous Reporter's account of the first battle was full of admiration and praise for the Yaqui braves: "These Indians fought as well and as energetically as any Indians I have seen since I have been in the Indies, and I have seen none fight better than they." Furthermore, he conceded, "if it were not for the flatness of the field on which

---

*Another common spelling for *Yaqui* in the Spanish and Jesuit records is *Hiaqui*. All archaic forms have been standardized in this text in the familiar, modern spelling of the name.

we fought, they would have inflicted even more damage to us, which was serious enough, for they wounded twelve horses and killed one, when we only had seventeen in all." That night in the Spanish camp, an old Yaqui presented himself to Captain Guzmán bearing a gift of three turquoise-studded maces. If these were meant to appease the foreigners and send them away, unfortunately they also confirmed Spanish suspicions of vast hidden treasures in the Yaqui villages. For the time being, however, the Yaquis' hostile reception discouraged Guzmán from pressing on. The Spaniards turned back for home, arriving at Culiacán on or shortly after Christmas to find their small settlement ravaged by recent Indian rebellions.

Besides reporting on the battle, the anonymous scribe also made some general observations which constituted the first known description of the Yaqui pueblos and their inhabitants. He noted that the Yaqui River "was populated with many people, and the pueblos are like those of the Sinaloa and the Mayo, although they are larger and better." The people, he continued, "make no sacrifices, nor have idols, but they worship the sun like heathens.... They work very hard because they hunt a lot." Finally, he compared the Yaqui language to German, perhaps a reference to the strangeness and difficulty of this new Indian tongue.[21]

An interval of ten years passed before the next documented Spanish–Yaqui encounter took place. During this time, several bands of Spanish explorers continued to push northward, but they either went around the Yaqui territory or traveled through so quickly that they aroused no notable reaction.

The second Spanish incident in the Yaqui River occurred as the culmination of one of the most bizarre and incredible adventures of the New World. Alvar Núñez Cabeza de Vaca and the three other sole survivors of the ill-fated Pánfilo de Narváez expedition to the Florida coast in 1527, having trekked westward through Texas and Chihuahua to the northern limits of Sonora, turned southward towards Culiacán at this point.[22] During the last leg of their long peregrination, accompanied by hundreds and thousands of friendly Indians who revered them as miracle healers, Cabeza de Vaca and his companions noted signs of Spanish presence. In Opata country of this middle Yaqui River, for example, he saw on the neck of an Indian "a little buckle from a swordbelt, and in it was sewn a horseshoe nail." Such a curious object could only have come from Spaniards he reasoned correctly. When pressed for further information, the Indians responded that men with beards had come from heaven to their homes and that they had horses, lances, and swords.

As the four wanderers pushed forward downriver, they arrived at the point "which Diego de Guzmán reached," Cabeza de Vaca noted retrospectively in his memoirs, and obtained definite news of the "Christians." The Yaquis appeared to him especially well off, for they were able to feed the Spaniards and their multitude of Indian companions "over two thousand loads of maize."[23] On the other hand, Cabeza de Vaca was deeply saddened by much of what he had seen in the territories recently explored and plundered by his countrymen. Many of the people had apparently deserted their homes and fields to flee to the mountains, in obvious fear of the white invaders and slave hunters. The situation worsened as he passed the Yaqui and approached the Fuerte River, for the ravages of Spanish slave and food raids from Culiacán were particularly glaring. So it was with mixed, bittersweet feelings that Cabeza de Vaca reunited with his fellow Spaniards at San Miguel de Culiacán in April 1536.

However, whatever shame or disappointment he might have felt about his compatriots' conduct towards the Indians did not dampen his own exuberant, and considerably exaggerated, reports of mountains covered with "gold, antimony, iron, copper and other metals" in that vast northern territory he had just traversed. His literally glittering accounts resuscitated interest in the search for gilded kingdoms, stimulating a new flurry of northward explorations. From 1540 to 1542, even the viceroy of New Spain, Antonio de Mendoza, personally financed an ambitious expedition, which he placed under the command of his nephew, Vázquez de Coronado. This party must have crossed the Yaqui River at some point, for it went as far north as the Missouri-Kansas line. But there is no record of unpleasant incidents with Indians in that vicinity.[24]

Coronado's voyage was the last expeditionary treasure hunt to the north; all hopeful Spaniards who had gone in search of El Dorado's elusive wealth and fame had returned empty-handed. Moreover, in 1542, the attention and limited resources of New Spain had to be directed to the pacification of the series of Indian uprisings in Nueva Galicia known as the Mixtón Wars.

Between 1542 and 1562, goaded not so much by visions of gilded kingdoms as gilded mines, the famed Basque prospector Diego de Ibarra and his nephew Francisco struck the rich silver veins of Zacatecas, Fresnillo, San Martín, Sombrerete, Nieves, Avinos, and others, all of which became overnight boom towns.[25] In July 1562, the still isolated and undefined territory north of the rapidly developing Nueva Galicia became the new political jurisdiction of Nueva Vizcaya, named after a Basque province. Appropriately, Francisco de Ibarra became its first governor and captain general.

Immediately upon assuming his new post, Ibarra turned his attention to the largely unexplored northwest, beginning with the province of Chiametla and moving northward to the region known as Sinaloa. By mid-1564, he had surveyed the Sinaloa and Fuerte rivers and founded the Spanish presidio settlement of San Juan de Carapoa, or San Juan de Sinaloa. Like his famous uncle Diego, Ibarra's primary purpose was to discover and exploit mines near settled Spanish locations and near sedentary Indians whose labor could be easily utilized.

Sometime in the spring or summer of 1565, towards the beginning of the rainy season, Francisco de Ibarra pushed still farther north beyond Sinaloa. His follower Balthasar de Obregón kept a meticulous chronicle of the expedition, which included an interesting encounter with Yaquis.[26] It was on the return trip from the Casas Grandes River in northwest Chihuahua that someone in Ibarra's party recalled the Yaqui River and suggested establishing a Spanish settlement among the Yaqui people. This time, the Spaniards approached the region from the Gulf of California. Perhaps informed of the unfortunate Diego de Guzmán incident many years earlier, Ibarra sent a messenger ahead to assure the Yaqui people of his peaceful coming. Obregón noted happily that the messengers "returned with good news. They said that the Yaquis were glad of the coming of the Christians. They promised a good reception for the general and his men."

True to their words, the Yaquis held a lavish and colorful reception for the visitors. As Obregón described it:

> At this welcome were five hundred handsome and brilliantly-dressed Indians. They wore their typical costumes, decorated with bright feathers, conches, beads and sea shells. They were well-equipped with weapons, although poor in clothing....

Ibarra in turn met the Yaquis "with much kindness and presented them with gifts."

Unlike the first encounter in 1533, Obregón observed the Yaquis at peace and leisure rather than at war. His effusive praise of the people and their settlements offer another view and convey some new impressions:

> This river of Yaquimí is the most thickly populated of all the regions traversed by the general. It must contain fifteen thousand men in the ten leagues from the sea to the mountain. The town is situated amid a luxuriant grove, a fourth of a league in extent. This river is large, cool, and contains quantities of good fish. On its margins are many fields of maize, beans and squashes. The people are kind. The women are beautiful and go about naked. Their long hair is worn loose and reaches to their waist. They cover their private parts with green grass. The general explored this river as far

as the sea. There we found clusters of coral and quantities of pearl-
bearing shells. The natives presented the Christians with gifts of
fish, game and other foods which they had in their land.

The image Obregón attempted to create was unmistakably that of a
bountiful, sensuous pagan paradise.

The good disposition of the people, the natural endowments of the
environment, all prompted Captain Ibarra to announce plans to build a
Spanish town in the Yaqui River. However, when the men he dispatched
to Sinaloa for "reinforcement of soldiers, implements, iron, ammunition
and moulds for adobe walls for building a fortress and founding a town"
returned empty-handed, Ibarra had to postpone the colonization project.
Apparently, the vecinos of Sinaloa were disappointed that Ibarra had
discovered no mines in the north. Moreover, they complained that they
had yet to receive their long promised *repartimiento,* or quota, of Indian
servants.

Ibarra left the Yaqui with firm intentions to return and settle it soon.
According to Obregón, Yaquis were saddened to see the Spaniards leave
and begged them to stay, promising to provide food for all as long as
they remained. Only reluctantly did they agree to provide Ibarra with
guides and armed escorts. Soon Spaniards understood why Yaquis were
so anxious for their friendship: it appeared that Yaquis were planning an
attack on the Mayos, their neighbor and current enemy to the south, and
hoped to make the white men their allies. Two thousand Yaquis who had
just executed a ceremonial farewell hunt and were still in war gears
insisted on accompanying the Spaniards on their journey home. "For this
reason," Obregón explained, "they treated us well, and the general kept
up the belief that he was going to aid them in war against their enemies."
As it turned out, it was just as well for the Spaniards that they had Yaquis
along, for "it was necessary to break through and open a road as we went
along, and even though the Indians helped, it [the terrain] was very
difficult to cross."

When Yaquis entered Mayo territory "with great determination and
courage," they plundered, killed, and destroyed the fields and homes of
their cowed enemies. It was with great effort that Ibarra finally prevailed
upon them to desist and make peace with the Mayos, and to exchange
bows and arrows to symbolize the end of hostilities.

After the Yaquis' departure, Ibarra explored the Mayo River and
found it equally as rich as the Yaqui. The wily general also made a pact
of friendship with the Mayos, promising "to come back to visit them
and to defend them against the damage inflicted by the people of the
Yaquimí." Obregón revealed that Yaquis were not only at war with

Mayos, but, in fact, were on hostile terms with all their surrounding neighbors, including the Uparos on the coast near the mouth of the Yaqui River and the Opatas and Nebomes up the river. By making these timely and separate friendship pacts with Yaquis and Mayos, Ibarra assured his own safety through this uncertain territory. Although clearly Yaquis implored Spaniards to stay because they saw in them valuable allies in war, it is doubtful whether they would have actually welcomed a permanent foreign settlement in their midst.

The history of Yaqui–Spanish contact during the sixteenth century did not follow a consistent, predictable pattern. Yaqui responses to Spanish intrusions appeared to have been dictated by practical assessments of threats and needs at a particular moment. The slave-raiding Nuño de Guzmán party, whose notoriety probably preceded their arrival, prompted Yaquis to repel them with determined force. Several decades later, when slaves raids had subsided, Francisco de Ibarra found a people poised for war and eager to win over Spaniards as allies. From the beginning, Yaquis demonstrated a practical flexibility and tended to seize the initiative in establishing their relationship with alien groups interested in them.

After Ibarra's brief sojourn and abortive attempt to found a Spanish settlement in the Yaqui River, no other Spanish party ventured that far north until the beginning of the seventeenth century. Spaniards were discouraged by their failure to locate the legendary kingdoms or civilizations with high material cultures; they were even more disappointed at not having discovered lucrative mines in the northwest. A further deterrent to continued northward expansion were the rebellions which broke out in Sinaloa. In 1569, the Suaquis of the Fuerte River, just south of the Mayo, rose up against the handful of Spanish colonists in San Juan de Carapoa, probably in reaction to the coercive encomienda system of labor and tribute. Later in the same century, this same people prevented Spaniards from resettling San Juan, forcing them to found a new town farther south on the Sinaloa River. San Felipe y Santiago contained a fort and a small garrison of twenty-five soldiers, the first presidio of the northwest frontier.[27]

At the end of the sixteenth century, the Fuerte River became an important demarcation between two zones: north of it, the indigenous population, which included the Yaquis, had largely escaped the institutions and ill effects of a permanent Spanish presence; south of it, the bulk of the population had been brought into the Spanish colonial system, and many of the communities had already begun to disintegrate. Some 8,000 Indians were paying tribute, close to half of them held in encomiendas.[28]

After more than half a century of exploration and colonization attempts in the northwest, Spaniards had only three rather miserable settlements to show for their efforts. All were located south of the Fuerte River: San Sebastián in Chiametla, San Miguel in Culiacán, and San Felipe in Sinaloa, the northernmost colony. The lingering prospect of striking gold or silver barely sustained the small group of vecinos in San Felipe, where Suaquis, Ocoronis, and Tehuecos constantly threatened their security. Until this frontier was pacified and the Indians made submissive to Spanish need for land and labor, the vecinos realized they could not hope to advance their interests in mining and cattle-raising, seen as the two great potentials of the north. Spaniards had also begun to understand that the operational methods which had proved so successful against the sedentary, advanced civilizations of central Mexico were not effective in the far more primitive north. They perceived correctly that this failure had much to do with the different stage of cultural development. Finally made aware of their own deficient human and material resources, Spaniards turned to missionaries for assistance in opening up this frontier.

CHAPTER 3

Enter the Jesuits

Ignatius Loyola founded the Company or Society of Jesus in 1534 explicitly for the purpose of converting "heathen souls" outside Europe to Christianity. It had already established considerable notoriety in the Far East before moving on to the New World, arriving in Mexico in 1572 as the last of four missionary orders.[1] For the first two decades, Jesuits occupied themselves mainly with priestly functions and educational endeavors in settled, urban Mexico, unable to penetrate the evangelical domain which Franciscans, Dominicans, and Augustinians had already monopolized from the Isthmus of Tehuantepec to Guanajuato. Finally, in 1587, the Crown granted Jesuits permission to pass to the still unpacified parts of the northern frontier, namely, the northwest and remote sections of the northeast.

Jesuits were not the first missionary order to operate in the northwest; Franciscans before them had shown great interest in Nueva Galicia and later Nueva Vizcaya. Several of the seekers for the illusory Cíbola were Franciscan friars, as were some of Francisco de Ibarra's companions on his various expeditions. As the northern frontier expanded, Franciscans eventually decided to concentrate their limited energies on the major mining zones of the northeast, thereby leaving the northwest wide open.[2] Into this remote, desolate vacuum stepped the Jesuits, eager for their own niche in New Spain.

Following the pattern they were establishing as they moved systematically northward, immediately upon their arrival at the Yaqui River in 1617, the Jesuit fathers quickly advanced beyond simple conversion to imposing profound changes on all aspects of Yaqui life and society. Within a short time, the early missionaries had transformed Yaqui culture from a loose federation of dispersed rancherías to a paragon of the Jesuit mission system. For the most part, the Yaqui people acquiesced in this directed cultural change, trading gains in economic security, political stability, and a better-defined identity for the loss of village autonomy. The Jesuits' phenomenal success in reorganizing almost all the indigenous nations of the northwest made the mission the dominant institution on the frontier, enabling Jesuits through their control of mission populations and economies to extend their hegemony over northwestern society in general.

From the outset, Jesuits distinguished themselves from the other orders. They did not subscribe to the Royal Patronage, whereby the King of Spain controlled ecclesiastical appointments and activities, but answered through their provincial in Mexico City to the general of their order in Rome and to the pope. This was to give rise to serious contentions between the Company and imperial authorities. Jesuits also realized from the very beginning that they operated in a missionary field quite different from central and southern New Spain. The indigenous peoples of their domain—the northern parts of Nayarit, most of Durango and Chihuahua, northern Sinaloa and all of Sonora and Baja California[3] — had an obviously different aboriginal culture and population distrubution pattern from the more advanced civilizations of Mesoamerica. The original plan conceived for all missionary orders was to reduce or congregate the Indians into villages for the purpose of conversion for ten-year grace periods; after that time, the converts were deemed fully prepared to take their proper place in colonial society and secularization was to take place. As secular priests replaced missionaries in the new parishes, Indians were assessed for tribute payment to the Crown. Jesuits felt strongly that this traditional plan of action had to be modified drastically to fit the conditions of the culturally less-developed north.

Herbert Eugene Bolton, the eminent frontier historian, described the purpose of the northern mission in these terms: "to check the evils of exploitation, and at the same time, to realize the ideals of conversion, protection and civilization." In other words, the mission was to serve the Church in converting "heathen souls" and the State in pacifying and civilizing the frontier, fulfilling in some ways the function of the encomienda, a transitional institution between conquest and colonization which Spaniards were unable to implant in the less sedentary and populated north. Originally the intention was also to secularize the northern missions after ten years of tutelage, but missionaries seldom, if ever, carried through this goal, contending that many more than ten years were necessary to civilize and stabilize the frontier.[4]

For the northwest then, Jesuits developed a new modus operandi, a special set of rules and precepts.[5] Instead of using the traditional terms of *pacification, reduction,* or *congregation* to describe their plan, they spoke rather of establishing "permanent missions among savages *(infieles)*." This expression embodied succinctly the paternalistic philosophy for which Jesuits were famous: that they were to define and assume responsibility for not only the spiritual, but also the social, political, and material needs of their Indian wards for an indefinite period of time. Mexican scholar Miguel Othón de Mendizábal argues that each Jesuit mission became, in effect, a "theocratic state" with absolute Jesuit control; another student of the system depicts the mission as a "community ruled by benign absolutism."[6]

In this extremely rational Jesuit schemework, each mission was coterminous with an indigenous nation. Some larger ones, such as the Yaqui, required the efforts of four or five missionaries; others, relatively small, could be easily administered by one father. The missionaries advanced cautiously, winning the loyalty of one nation before moving on to the next, never overextending their available human and material resources. Instead of building grandiose churches or lavish monasteries, delivering eloquent public sermons, or mounting impressive mass baptisms, they concentrated first on doctrinal education for adults in the native tongues and on economic reorganization.[7]

A firm economic base was the foundation of the Jesuit mission system. The missionaries realized that, just as initial conversion was facilitated "through the mouth," so only by the same means could they ensure permanence and stability. Furthermore, economically sound missions could support the founding of new ones in stretching the seemingly elastic frontier of the Jesuit empire.

Another significant consequence of Jesuit reorganization was the reinforcement or, in many cases, the creation of a sense of community — a political and cultural unity among rancherías speaking the same language and sharing the same social development. In the case of the Yaquis, their culture and identity as modified by the mission system actually supplanted most traces and erased most memories of their aboriginal or pre-Jesuit past.

For a century after the Jesuits' arrival in the northwest, their pre-eminence withstood all challenges from the small, struggling Spanish communities around them. At the same time, their phenomenal evangelical and economic successes in the missions only accentuated the concurrent retardation of Spanish colonization. Their critics charged that Jesuits had translated the ideal of "checking the evils of exploitation" into a near monopoly which made it extremely difficult for fledgling Spanish miners, hacendados, and merchants to compete equally for Indian land, labor, produce, and markets. The sharply defined political conflict between Spaniards and Jesuits centered around the controversial question of secularization.

The balance of power began to shift towards the end of the seventeenth century, with the discovery of important mines in Sonora and Sinaloa. As Spanish society and economy finally began to develop in a significant way, so too did the vecinos' ability to compete for Indian resources improve. Increased pressures from both secular and religious quarters led to a series of devastating Indian rebellions in the northwest during the eighteenth century, the 1740 Yaqui uprising being one of the worst. Actually, well before this time in other parts of the north serious rebellions had already occurred; in the northwest the inevitable clash between mission and mine was delayed, but not forestalled forever. These violent confrontations began to undermine the carefully constructed Jesuit hegemony, signalling the onset of Jesuit decline.

The Yaqui Mission

The first two Jesuits arrived in Sinaloa in 1591, followed shortly by five more. A garrison of twenty-five presidial soldiers under the command of the indefatigable Captain Diego Martínez de Hurdaide protected and assisted them in every way.[8] Headquartered at the new fort of San Felipe, these soldiers served as a vanguard for the advancing missionaries, clearing the way each step northward. By 1606, the Jesuits had fully missionized the nations of the Fuerte River, reporting at that time over 40,000 converts, out of a total estimated population of 100,000.[9] Evangelical eyes then turned with much anticipation to the last two great rivers of Sinaloa, the Mayo and the Yaqui.

As early as 1605, Father Juan de Velasco, who was then at work on a primer of the Cáhita language, might have visited the Mayo people and received their request for missionaries.[10] Hemmed in between two persistent adversaries, the Yaquis to the north and the Tehuecos to the south,

Mayos could well have sought missionary presence as a safeguard against further attacks. Before the fathers could attend to them, however, the missionized Ocoronis of the Fuerte River rebelled. Both Jesuits and civil authorities were anxious to suppress the uprising before it could spread to other areas in Sinaloa. In spite of their precautions, Ocoroni agitators penetrated the Yaqui River, winning the support of several rancherías and provoking the first serious Spanish–Yaqui encounter since Ibarra. Jesuit missionary records are the only known source of information on the ensuing protracted confrontation between Captain Hurdaide and the Yaquis. Even though the picture is rather one-sided, still it is important to examine this series of violent incidents as the prelude to the eventual peaceful entrance of Jesuits to the Yaqui River.

Leader of the Ocoroni rebels who fled inland to the Yaqui was Juan Lautaro, described as "very astute, clever and *ladino,*" meaning acculturated, the consequence of his employment in the Spanish mining town of San Andres in the Sierra Madre.[11] Although Yaquis had had no previous contact with Ocoronis, they succumbed to Lautaro's charismatic leadership; he must have convinced them that Spanish proximity posed a clear and present danger to their security and welfare.

Unrest among the Yaquis forced Hurdaide to move prematurely to that region, even though Jesuits were not quite ready to missionize the Yaqui nation, having not yet secured the Mayos. At first Hurdaide tried to persuade Yaquis to renounce Lautaro and cohorts. When this overture failed, he still did not wish to seek open hostility with the populous and much-feared Yaquis, since he had only 400 men between Spaniards and Indian auxiliaries. So for the second time, Hurdaide extended peace feelers to the Yaquis; he felt somewhat encouraged when a principal named Anabailutei visited him at San Felipe with offers to cooperate. By mutual agreement, the captain sent several Christianized Tehueco Indians with the Yaqui leader to pick up the Ocoroni troublemakers. He also sent along two captured Yaqui women who had been converted and baptized in San Felipe, hoping that they too would exert a "Christian" influence on their own people. Unfortunately for Hurdaide, Anabailutei was unable to keep his word, for apparently he did not act with the consensus of his people. Upon approaching the Yaqui territory, some Yaquis pounced on the hapless Tehuecos, robbing them of their clothing and horses before killing them. This unprovoked act of violence in turn aroused the furor of the Tehuecos, who clamored for revenge. The credibility and reputation of all Spaniards now at stake, Captain Hurdaide finally felt obliged to take punitive action. In addition to his 40 mounted men, he raised an auxiliary force of 2,000 Indians, among them many Mayos.

The Yaquis responded to Hurdaide's armed advance with a furious assault, killing a good number of Mayo and Tehueco auxiliaries and seriously wounding several Spaniards with their poisonous arrows. With food running short and the wounded requiring treatment, Hurdaide ordered the retreat to San Felipe, vowing to return soon with a larger force to suppress the rebels once and for all.

Reinforced with additional troops from Culiacán, Hurdaide launched another punitive expedition against the Yaquis. And again, Yaquis humiliated the captain, sending his 50 mounted and 400 Indian foot soldiers scurrying through a dense forest in all directions. Sometime during this chaotic battle, Hurdaide and his rearguard separated from his vanguard, which retreated hastily to San Felipe bearing the dire news of the captain's presumed death.

Actually Hurdaide and twenty-five men had withdrawn for refuge to a treeless hillock overlooking the Yaqui River. Wounded, hungry, and without gunpowder, they sucked on lead bullets to relieve the thirst caused by a scorching sun. To make their misery worse, several thousand Yaquis deliberately cavorted before their eyes in the refreshingly cool water of the river. Only by using his wits did Hurdaide save himself and his men from this hopeless situation. That night, he sent galloping frantically towards the river the weakest of their horses; as predicted and hoped, Yaquis gave chase to the animals, thus affording the Spaniards their chance to flee on the healthier horses. Both Hurdiade and the missionaries were thankful that the Sinaloa Indians did not rebel during his absence.

His limited resources now exhausted and no new aid forthcoming—indeed, his superior, the governor of Nueva Vizcaya, actually reprimanded him for his latest ventures—Hurdaide could not possibly undertake another armed expedition. Once again, he outwitted his adversaries, this time circulating alarming rumors throughout Sinaloa that the colonial government was planning an enormous military invasion of the Yaqui. Conveniently for Hurdaide, by coincidence a pearl-fishing boat was cruising the Sinaloa coast at this time, thereby confirming for the Yaquis the disquieting reports. To top off his scheme, Hurdaide embellished it with additional rumors of three squadrons already poised for the attack on the Yaqui River. Finally, he let it be known widely that all the Indian nations desiring to settle old scores with Yaquis would be invited to join the invasion.

The ruse worked, and Yaquis sued for peace. Although they had repelled successive Spanish assaults and inflicted heavy casualties on the unmounted Indian auxiliaries, they had not captured a single Spanish prisoner of war or killed a single mounted soldier. Moreover, they were troubled by Hurdaide's mysterious escape. Jesuits concluded that Yaquis were morally discouraged by these signs of Spanish invincibility. Captain Hurdaide invited Yaqui leaders to visit San Felipe and negotiate the terms of peace with him personally. He demanded that peaceful Yaquis return to their homes, so that he could tell them apart from the recalcitrant handful who had fled to the sierra. He also required them not to wage war against Mayos or any other neighbor. Finally, he asked the surrendered Yaquis to imprison or kill Lautaro and the other leaders of the resistance. For his part, he promised to aid Yaquis in case they were attacked by any group.

On 25 April 1610, one hundred and fifty Yaqui representatives observed the formal signing of the peace in San Felipe. Jesuit fathers showered the visitors with gifts, lavish praises, and invitations to several youths to attend the missionary school in Culiacán. Furthermore, they promised to send missionaries to the Yaquis as soon as new personnel arrived. During the next few years, small contingents of curious Yaquis made sporadic visits to San Felipe, keeping in touch with their erstwhile enemies turned friends.[12]

The successful peace negotiations largely restored Hurdaide's dwindling prestige. His defeats at Yaqui hands were the only ones he suffered during a long career of opening up the northwestern frontier for the Jesuits. In taking on the famed Yaqui warriors, the capitán simply did not bargain for such formidable foes.

Jesuit accounts of these episodes did not contain much analysis of Yaqui motives, first for waging relentless war against Spaniards, then suing for peace after apparent victories. Given past Yaqui reactions to outside encroachments, however, their decisions were not too difficult to understand. At first, it seems, Yaquis perceived a real threat in the steady northward advance of Spaniards and missionaries, an attitude similar to the one they had exhibited towards Diego de Guzmán in 1533. The Ocoroni fugitives activated latent apprehensions. But after the rather hollow victories over a determined and clever Captain Hurdaide, Yaqui pragmatism and flexibility prevailed, prompting them to choose peace over a futile, protracted struggle. Yaquis might also have learned that Spanish presence meant essentially two or three unarmed, peaceful missionaries, not whole settlements of rapacious foreign intruders.

In the same year of the peace, the presidial outpost at San Felipe moved one river north to the newly constructed Fort of Montesclaros on the Suaqui River, henceforth renamed the Fuerto (Fort) River. The Yaquis' unexpected strength had convinced the viceroy of the necessity of taking this step in order to fortify frontier defenses. Also in the same year, rebellious Xiximees submitted peacefully to the Spaniards, who had just suppressed a Tehueco uprising. With the reputation of the missionaries rapidly spreading, Nebomes, Nures, Tepahues, and other nations asked for their presence.[13]

In 1614, Jesuits were ready to carry the cross to the Mayos, the last stepping stone on the way to the great Yaqui nation. The Mayos had generally been friendly to Spaniards and had served willingly in several of Hurdaide's auxiliary forces even before conversion. When the captain and Father Pedro Méndez arrived at the Mayo, they found the river in a desperate state of famine. The capitán immediately sent for relief provisions from the neighboring Nebomes and Nures. This timely aid further facilitated the already assured establishment of the Mayo mission.[14] By 1620 Méndez and his associate had reduced the entire Mayo population of around 20,000 to six permanent pueblos on the last ten leagues of the Mayo River.[15]

Besides the successful conversion of the Mayos, another event hastened the advent of Jesuits to the Yaqui. In 1616, the Tepehuanes carried out a premeditated uprising in the major mining zone of the Sierra Madre. This rebellion, which some Jesuit historians have considered "the most serious revolt in the history of the missions of Mexico," was the Tepehuanes' reaction against intolerable pressures from two sources: the Jesuit mission system and the Spanish mining society. Despite Jesuit warnings to leave the Indians "in peace," miners continued to recruit and coerce Tepehuanes to work for them. When the Indians finally exploded, they killed all foreigners in sight, making no distinction between missionaries and miners, and destroyed mission pueblos and churches as well as mining towns.[16]

Tepehuan overtures to Yaquis caused much alarm for Hurdaide and Jesuits, who concluded that the only insurance against further disturbances in the northwestern frontier was to convert and missionize the Yaquis immediately and peacefully. While the captain busied his troops with sealing off the west side of the Sierra Madre from the volatile Tepehuan rebellion, Jesuits prepared to move northward again.[17]

On Ascension Day, 20 May 1617, having mapped out their course of action and brushed up on their Cáhita, the veteran missionary Andrés Pérez de Ribas and the young Tomás Basilio left the Mayo mission for the Yaqui River.[18] Deviating notably from the established pattern and assuming obvious risks, but anxious to Christianize the unpredictable Yaquis without delay, the two fathers went without the customary escort of Captain Hurdaide. Preoccupied elsewhere, the captain could not spare himself or any of his men. Despite the absence of presidial escorts, the Jesuits traveled to the Yaqui with the usual large entourage of Indians, including converted Suaquis who were to act as their apostolic assistants and Yaqui caciques who had journeyed earlier to the Mayo to lead the way. Hence the missionaries' duly heralded arrival caused no unpleasant surprise and prompted no organized hostility.[19] The fathers entered the Yaqui from the first hamlet upriver, where some 200 people had gathered to greet them, some enthusiastically waving homemade cane crosses. Pérez de Ribas was immediately impressed with the size of the Yaqui River, nostalgically comparing it to the Guadalquivir River of his native Andalucia. Although he christened it the *Espíritu Santo,* or Holy Spirit, Jesuits and others continued to use the familiar name of Yaqui.

At the first stop, the fathers established a clear procedural pattern which they followed closely in all the other ten rancherías they visited downriver. First, gathering the curious crowd around an *enramada* or hut which served as a temporary chapel, Father Pérez de Ribas explained their purpose and delivered a brief sermon on the Christian doctrines. Then, as was customary missionary practice, he and Basilio baptized all children under seven, reported at around 200, while putting off the ceremony for adults until they had acquired more doctrinal instruction. After three days, the two Jesuits passed on to the next stop, to which over 1,000 families had flocked. Here they baptized another 200 or more children, causing Pérez de Ribas to feign desperation for having exhausted his stock of good Christian names: already, he lamented with good humor, he had assigned Juan and Pedro many times over. In these first baptisms, the Christian Suaquis stood as *padrinos* or godfathers.[20]

A few unpleasant incidents marred an otherwise most propitious beginning. Friendly Yaquis warned the fathers that from the fifth settlement on, the people would no longer be so open and enthusiastic about their coming. But when the missionaries arrived at the fifth ranchería, called Abasórin, they encountered an even larger gathering of onlookers than they previously had seen. These lower communities appeared more populous, ranging in size from 600 to 1,000 households each. At Abasórin, the first of three abortive attempts at the Jesuits' lives occurred. An urgent call for Father Basilio to attend to a sick man downriver turned out to be a trick to lure him away from the large crowd so that he could be murdered. Fortunately, friendly Yaquis warned the fathers of the plot in time; others tried to dissuade them from continuing their journey. By this time, Pérez de Ribas had clearly perceived discord between the two halves of the river concerning their presence and activities. This only made him all the more determined to proceed as planned, in order to prove to the skeptics his sincerity and faith. That two other attempts at their lives ended similarly in failure translated into a good omen for the deeply committed fathers.

As they continued on to Tórin, the sixth pueblo, they found as expected that not everyone from the 1,000 and more families of this reputedly most bellicose community had come out to greet them. But the opportune friendship of one of Tórin's most respected residents guaranteed their safety. At Tórin and the last three rancherías they visited, the fathers baptized over 3,000 children.[21] Upon the conclusion of this introductory tour, Pérez de Ribas pronounced the initial conversion of the largest nation of Sinaloa the most "resplendant" so far.[22]

Father Pérez de Ribas's memoirs constitute the only source on the Jesuits' first experiences in the Yaqui River; all other and later summaries are based on this primary account. However, the eminent Jesuit composed his work many years after he had left the Yaqui mission; hence much of what took place he described in vague, general, or incomplete terms. For example, he rounded out population figures to the nearest hundred or thousand, and left out crucial dates and place names at frequent points of his recollection. He also tended to simplify and overgeneralize the Yaquis' initial reactions. Then when he was forced to admit that perhaps not all Yaquis were equally elated about their presence, he blamed it on what he thought to be the pernicious influence of the hechiceros, the one group which he singled out for special attention and condemnation.

Father Pérez de Ribas discerned an hechicero conspiracy against the missionary enterprise, attributing to it every reluctant gesture — a mother who hesitated to have her children baptized — every cool glance, every hostile move, especially the three murder plots. His fear eventually led to unreason when he even accused the hechiceros of masterminding a smallpox epidemic which broke out in the Yaqui soon after his arrival. If somewhat exaggerated, Pérez de Ribas's preoccupation was not totally unfounded. As religious and ritual specialists, hechiceros came closest to a professional priesthood in aboriginal Yaqui society, the group with the greatest incentive to compete with missionaries for the people's faith, confidence, and respect. Jesuits quickly deemed imperative the neutralization of the hechiceros' power and prestige. They also astutely coupled the antihechicero campaign with open courtship of other community leaders in order to expedite winning over the rest of the population and to protect themselves against possible hechicero wrath.[23]

As it turned out, hechiceros were unable to mount any serious effort to drive the Jesuits out. Arriving unarmed, unescorted by soldiers, and fully expected in advance, the two fathers constituted no threat to the Yaqui rancherías in any traditional sense. Under these circumstances, it would have been very difficult for any one ranchería, individual, or group, including the hechiceros, to mobilize the rest of the population to repel apparently harmless visitors. In the particular case of the hechiceros, they did not constitute a ruling elite in a society which had so such class; hence they had no institutionalized collective power or responsibility for the welfare of their people. Rather, they acted as individuals with bases only in their respective rancherías. So even if some hechiceros did respond negatively to missionary intrusion into their spiritual domain, they would have experienced difficulty generalizing their opposition beyond strictly person and local bounds. In time, hechiceros learned to exist unobtrusively alongside Jesuits, and Jesuits came to tolerate their increasingly innocuous existence. Few missionaries since Pérez de Ribas ever brought up the hechicero issue again.

As soon as they had settled in, Fathers Pérez de Ribas and Basilio unfolded their mission blueprint. First of all, they had Indian assistants from established missions transport prodigious quantities of food to the new mission site. They needed these provisions to entice Yaquis from distant, dispersed rancherías to leave their homes and fields to take up new residence in the eleven settlements along the river. While this relocation was still taking place, the fathers directed the construction of the first churches, keeping the laborers well fed from the imported stock.[24]

Next the Jesuits proceeded to stamp out what they considered to be heathen customs and to preach against the influence of hechiceros. Pérez de Ribas described vividly some of the "barbarian" practices and rituals; these included wild, drunken orgies, lewd dancing with scalps of Mayo captives, shameless polygamy, and crude superstitions.

The fathers experienced relative ease in imposing the new religion upon the ruins of the old. Suaqui catechists and Yaqui youths educated at the San Felipe Jesuit college ably assisted them in doctrinal education for adults. Caciques who were baptized first stood as padrinos for the others who followed their example. The process went so smoothly that Pérez de Ribas jubilantly reported at the end of the first six months the baptism of 5,000 children and 3,000 adults. Yaquis also responded well to Jesuit peace-making efforts, to the point of inviting some hard-pressed Guaymas Indians to move into their pueblos, till their land, in short, become part of the new mission community.[25]

These auspicious beginnings beckoned Captain Hurdaide in 1618 to venture into his old battleground for a peaceful visit. The Jesuits also hoped that an impressive parade in full military regalia would help unnerve the still dissident elements. During his pleasant tour, Hurdaide introduced the rudiments of Spanish civil government by appointing the first Yaqui *gobernadores* and *alcaldes*. Although in theory these secular officials were to answer directly to him, in practice he left it up to the fathers to define their specific duties, to appoint their assistants, and to supervise their performances in office.

Before Pérez de Ribas could witness the stabilization of the Yaqui mission, he was called to assume higher administrative duties in Mexico City. Father Basilio remained to assist the new head missionary, Father Cristóbal de Villalta, and to welcome additional companions, Fathers Pedro Méndez and Angelo Balestra, both veterans of the Mayo mission, and the newly arrived Juan de Ardeñas.[26]

Around the time of Pérez de Ribas's departure, the Mayo, Yaqui, and Nebome missions were made into a new administrative subdivision, the *rectorado* of San Ignacio. These new missions were considered too distant from the vice-provincial at San Felipe for his effective supervision. Headquartered at the Yaqui with Father Villalta as superior, the rectorado San Ignacio claimed a combined total population of almost 60,000 —30,000 in the Yaqui mission, 20,000 in the Mayo, and 9,000 in the Nebome.[27] By 1623, according to Jesuit records, missionaries had baptized "all the Yaquis."[28] The Yaqui mission appeared to have been fully stabilized.

A fully established mission was a complex and extremely well organized institution. In the Yaqui, full conversion entailed the further reduction of the eleven congregations along the river to eight permanent pueblos.[29] These have continued as Yaqui villages ever since, the term *Eight Pueblos* having become synonymous with the Yaqui nation. Their significance is underscored by the fact that the history of their founding, rather than the eighty or so original rancherías, form the basis of the Yaqui myth of creation, which recounts in legendary fashion how eight different tribes settled in the Yaqui River and eventually merged into the Yaqui people.[30] From upriver to the coast, these pueblos bear the elaborate names of: Espíritu Santo de Cócorit, Santa Rosa de Bácum, San Ignacio de Tórin, La Natividad del Señor de Vícam, La Santísima Trinidad de Pótam, La Asunción de Ráum; Santa Bárbara de Huírivis, and San Miguel de Belém.[31] The Christian parts of these cumbersome names have seldom been used, so that from the beginning they have not been commonly known. All except Belém were originally on the left bank of the river, but through the years the changing course of the waterway has caused the relocation of some of these pueblos.

These eight were further divided into four *partidos* of two villages each; the *cabecera,* or head mission pueblo, housed a resident missionary who also attended to the *pueblo de visita,* or affiliate. Father Superior Villalta resided in Tórin, the cabecera of the Yaqui mission as well as of the rectorado San Ignacio. Each one of the eight Yaqui villages boasted a church. The Indians built new homes for themselves as well as for the fathers, who reported with great pride that:

> The pueblos are in very good condition, and no one any longer lives in his field or any old ranchería. The houses are also in good shape, being made of adobe and roofed.... The padres also have adequate houses.[32]

Unlike congregations in the center and south of New Spain, Jesuits did not lay out the mission pueblos according to the Spanish grid plan. Instead, they allowed the residents of the relatively small pueblos to group their new homes in an irregular fashion around the churches.[33] These eight mission centers not only enabled the four or five resident missionaries to maintain almost daily contact with the converts, but also formed the basis for the next important tasks, political and economic reorganization.

To begin with, Jesuits elaborated upon the skeletal foundation of civil government which Hurdaide had laid in 1618, adding a few religious offices of their own. Each pueblo acquired its own set of magistrates, whose duties as Jesuits defined them were:

> to assist the missionary in fulfilling his office, to share with him in the supervision and care of the Indians, and by vigilance, by the good reputation they enjoyed, and by their good example, to keep the other Indians in good order.[34]

In view of these heavy responsibilities, the fathers explained, they made sure to select for public service elders or principales "who seemed also to be true and pious Christians."[35] In other words from the very beginning Jesuits violated the Yaquis' right to elections out of distrust for their judgment.

The first and most prestigious official of each pueblo was the gobernador.[36] As the civil authority's nominal representative in the mission, in theory his duties were "to pass judgement on disputes which occurred in the village, to see that the laws were obeyed, and to punish transgressions according to their seriousness." Adopting a custom from Yaqui tradition, he held as symbol of authority "a staff ... fitted with a silver knob weighing a pound."[37] In practice, however, the resident missionary considerably curtailed the gobernador's power, compelling the native magistrate to answer directly to him rather than to Sinaloa's captain-general. Without his prior consent the gobernador could not mete out serious punishments.[38]

The alcalde was the gobernador's right-hand man, assisting him in all his duties, carrying out his orders, and substituting for him in his absence.[39] In the seventeenth century there were no other civil officials in the Yaqui mission. Unlike later missions established on the dangerous Apache frontier of the Pimería Alta, the early Yaqui mission existed within the bounds of a pacific Jesuit domain. With no constant threat to their security, these Sinaloa missions consequently felt little need for military positions. The situation would change in the next century.

The missionaries did create a set of religious officials to assist them in spiritual and church-related matters. Chief among them was the *fiscal de iglesia,* who aided the resident father in all his duties, sometimes even taking over in the father's absence. The missionary described the fiscal as his eyes and ears,

> responsible for reporting everything that had to do with the church, people who wanted to be married, baptisms of newborns, fiestas they wanted to celebrate, sick people who needed the sacraments, accompanying the fathers on their visits to the pueblos, or otherwise taking care of any necessity, informing the people of the laws and warning them of any violation of Christian customs.[40]

The fiscal summoned the people for assemblies to discuss a community project or to make a general announcement. As the missionary's spy, he noted down the names of those who failed to attend Sunday masses and important feast days and reported transgressors of the law for proper punishment. These broad responsibilities often placed fiscales in positions of confidence with missionaries, their influence perhaps superseding the gobernadores' authority. They also held a staff of office.[41]

Other church officials known generally as *temastianes* performed a variety of services. Those acting as catechists, sometimes called *madores,* supervised the doctrinal instruction of older children and made sure they attended mass.[42] Sacristans took care of the ornaments and conditions of the churches, especially during fiestas.

Besides their handsome staffs, all Indian officials received special vestments to distinguish them from the common people. Gobernadores sometimes also enjoyed bigger houses.[43]

Installment of these village administrative bodies within the Yaqui mission displaced the traditional community councils. Elders and principales gave way to gobernadores and fiscales. Although Jesuits occasionally assembled the community for announcements, they did not as a rule consult the people before taking important decisions.

Still there is no record of Yaquis expressing grave reservations about these political innovations. The Jesuits' astute policy of elevating existing elders to the new positions of authority undoubtedly limited opposition and facilitated the transition. At the same time, just as they quickly eliminated hechiceros as ritual specialists, the missionaries excluded them from participation in the new system. Most importantly, Jesuits quietly inserted themselves as the supreme authority within the mission. They resolved all major disputes between individuals and introduced corporal punishment to reinforce discipline. Not surprisingly, Pérez de Ribas maintained that Yaquis generally preferred to approach missionaries with their problems rather than appeal to the native magistrates.[44] Instead of holding popular elections, as Hurdaide had originally instructed, Jesuits did not hide the fact that they actually designated the candidates for each office in order to ensure the choice of tractable, loyal, and obedient servants. As one father explained matter-of-factly: "The ministering father guides the people in this election so that they may give their votes to someone whose conduct of life will not serve as a stumbling block but as a check upon evil and a spur for all good."[45] There could be no clearer expression of Jesuit paternalism.

Jesuit educational policy also betrayed their strong paternalistic inclinations. They distinguished between different types of education: doctrinal instruction was deemed imperative; cultural instruction, including music, was considered desirable.[46] However, they thought it superfluous, if not dangerous, to teach Yaquis the Spanish language, for such knowledge would facilitate their communication with the outside Spanish world. This imposed language barrier fostered a dependency that allowed missionaries — all of whom were required to master the native tongues — to assume the critical role of cultural broker for the Indians, filtering and interpreting for them only what they considered desirable about Spanish secular culture.

Further reinforcing the mission as a theocratic state was the Jesuits' economic reorganization of native society.[47] In their self-delegated roles as planners and managers, Jesuits again assumed supreme authority. Their goal in each mission was to achieve economic self-sufficiency and stability, to eliminate totally the need to hunt and gather, in short, to reach the level of substantial surplus production. The first missionaries recognized the Yaquis as basically *labradores,* or cultivators. They also saw that Yaquis were not exploiting to the fullest extent the potential of their rich and naturally well-irrigated valley land. So they based the new economic system on a more rational utilization of available land, water, and labor. The missionaries assigned each family in the eight pueblos a plot of land, which it worked three out of the six weekly workdays and consumed what it produced.[48] Then they required all able-bodied men to spend the other three working days cultivating communal plots, an innovation designed to produce food for the missionaries and to ensure a surplus. Gobernadores and alcaldes assisted the resident fathers in supervising what was surely the first systematic collective economic activity in Yaqui history.[49]

Missionaries introduced other new practices. They taught Yaquis how to husband their foodstuff, that is, to save from one harvest to the next and to reserve seeds for the next planting.[50] They installed systems of artificial irrigation and water control, such as canals and dams. They replaced the traditional digging stick with the European hoe and brought in other new farming techniques and new crops, such as wheat, barley, and oats.[51] Father Pérez de Ribas personally introduced cows, burros, cattle, and sheep to start a grazing industry; horses left by the first Spaniards were already multiplying on Yaqui pastures when Jesuits arrived.[52] Tended by families and on communal ranches, these animals substantially augmented and improved the Yaqui diet, as well as contributed to the general surplus. Under Jesuit tutelage and management, Yaqui productivity increased significantly within a short time.

The economic surplus became the hallmark of the Yaqui and other Indian missions, as well as the source of bitter controversies. In answer to their critics, Jesuits vehemently denied that they ever exploited Indians for unpaid labor in the missions, arguing strenuously that communal fruits benefitted everyone equally. They pointed out that surpluses fed the laborers during the three communal workdays and nourished widows, orphans, the old and infirm, and others incapable of producing for themselves, including sometimes presidial soldiers, unconverted Indians found wandering near the missions, and those serving full time in civil and religious offices.[53]

Also hotly debated was the Jesuit practice of selling part of the surplus to clients outside the missions and using the money earned to buy items not manufactured within the pueblos. Jesuit agents in Mexico City bought garments for the scantily clad Indians, as well as tobacco, medicines, agricultural implements, church ornaments, candles and wine for the Mass, and many other such essentials.[54] At the same time, the fathers prohibited Indians from trading directly with Spaniards.

The surplus was also important as a reserve of grains and cattle in case of natural disasters. One good measure of a mission's success and security was its ability to care for its people during times of crisis. The missionaries were most concerned about floods or droughts which disrupted the normal cycle of cultivation or destroyed unharvested crops, leading to famine. If these crises were not successfully bridged, it could mean the end of a mission's existence. Some of the poorer Sinaloan missions reported famines which forced their Indians to leave their homes and revert to hunting and gathering in the mountains.[55] During the entire seventeenth century, Jesuits in the prosperous Yaqui mission never allowed food shortages to plunge the people into total despair leading to desertion of their pueblos. In 1655, for example, when a great flood caused the damage of cultivated fields, resident fathers doled out a prodigious amount of food from the communal granaries. In two pueblos alone, Ráum and Pótam, they handed out over 6,000 rations of food each day for four months.[56] This feat attested to an impressive abundance of surplus food in the Yaqui mission, the result of bountiful harvests and astute Jesuit management.

Finally, the surplus was indispensable in the continuous extention of the Jesuit mission system northward.

Besides improving agriculture as a means to self-sufficiency, Jesuits also encouraged the growth and development of native arts and crafts. They served as master teachers for new trades and skills. When Pérez de Ribas noticed that Yaqui women knew some rudimentary weaving, he not only urged the continuation of this industry but the expanded cultivation of cotton as well. Later he was able to remark with much pride that "the Yaqui women were great weavers and wove beautiful cloths to cover themselves." Carpenters, shoemakers, blacksmiths, tailors, painters, all opened shops in the pueblos.

With only minimal help from the Crown, the missions sustained themselves almost solely by their own products. Although since 1592 each missionary in the field was entitled to a yearly royal stipend of 300 pesos, more often than not this subvention never arrived. Private donations also did not amount to much for the remote Sinaloa and Sonora missions. The most valuable impetus the Crown could give the northern missions was to exempt them from any kind of taxation, the same exemption granted all Indian reductions in New Spain normally for ten years, at most twenty. In the northwest, Jesuits managed to prolong this privilege far beyond the usual allotted time span. In fact, the Yaqui and other missions never paid any taxes at all. What would have been lost in taxation accrued to the mission coffers instead. Jesuits fought long and hard to keep Yaquis under perpetual tutelage, the official status under which Indians could remain free from the onus of tribute.

In summarizing the Jesuit efforts at reorganizing Yaqui society, there is no record of serious discontentment or widespread resistance to the changes. Even if Jesuits were prone to minimize conflicts, secular authorities would have reported major disturbances, since they were responsible for suppressing them. Such was the case, for example, with the 1616 Tepehuan rebellion, which was exhaustively discussed in both

Jesuit and secular sources of Nueva Vizcaya. It appeared that Jesuits successfully established the Yaqui mission primarily through persuasion and demonstration, resorting minimally if at all to force or coercion. It is difficult to conceive how four or five unarmed and unescorted missionaries could have convinced 30,000 cautious Yaquis to submit to their paternalistic rule other than by peaceful means. The classless nature of aboriginal Yaqui society meant that Jesuits encountered no powerful native ruling elite to combat, destroy, and replace. The absence of a competitive secular society for most of the seventeenth century also contributed to the relatively low level of tension in the general environment.

For their part, Yaquis apparently assessed the Jesuit reordering to be generally beneficial to their daily well-being and overall security. The creation of eight close-knit mission pueblos out of eighty scattered autonomous rancherías produced a greatly heightened sense of unity, solidarity, territoriality, and cultural identity among the 30,000 Yaquis, in short, a deeper consciousness of being one people.

Jesuits were so pleased with their achievement that they considered the Yaqui mission their showcase in the entire northwest by midseventeenth century;[57] but this euphoria was not to last forever. The steady growth of secular society on the frontier during the eighteenth century introduced new tensions that disrupted the splendid isolation and harmonious relationships of the missions. Fighting hard to preserve their hegemony, missionaries were tormented by the problem of protecting their Indians physically and morally from the encroaching Spaniards. Yaquis found themselves caught in the midst of an accelerating conflict which they had absolutely no part in forming.

Sinaloa and Sonora: The Northwest Secular Society

The kingdom of Nueva Vizcaya, created in 1562, originally covered all of New Spain's northern frontier. Its governor was also the captain-general, subordinate to the viceroy in political matters but to the Audiencia (High Court) of Guadalajara in judicial matters. Although the seat of government was formally at Durango (Guadiana), where the bishop also maintained his official headquarters, the governor often preferred to preside in the important mining town of Parral. The society was a simplified one, consisting of missions, presidios, reales de minas, and administrative towns. The mission was the only stable and permanent institution, whereas the others, constituting Spanish society, were uncertain and ephemeral. Presidios moved with the frontier; reales endured only as long as mineral deposits lasted; administrative centers often coincided with reales.

Jesuits readily deprecated the small secular population outside their missions: "Practically all those who wished to be considered Spaniards were people of mixed bloods.... There was hardly a true Spaniard.[58] They were quite correct in pointing out that the secular society was really a Spanish-speaking non-Indian world that included many mestizos and mulattoes. The growth of this motley population was slow and painful. As late as 1693, Joseph Francisco Marín, viceregal inspector for Nueva Vizcaya, noted the existence of some 150 Indian nations, but only about 500 Spaniards, most of them struggling miners, hacendados, and merchants.[59] Almost all their activities were geared to the functioning and support of the mines.

Throughout the frontier region, Spanish entrepreneurs exerted pressures on mission Indians to work in their mines and related agricultural and ranching activities. Such demands were largely responsible for the devastating 1616 Tepehuan rebellion. Obviously, mines could not be worked without a steady supply of cheap laborers. So despite the royal *cédulas* which specifically prohibited Indian slavery, except those captured in "just wars," and despite the close vigilance of the Jesuits, Indians continued to be "captured and taken as slaves — sold or given away — in the mines."[60] Since civil administrators and presidial captains often connived in this constant search for manpower, they obviously did not enforce the laws vigorously.

In the seventeenth century, an even more simplified Spanish society was found in the northwestern provinces of Sinaloa and Sonora, governed jointly as one administrative subdivision of Nueva Vizcaya by an official holding both the alcalde-mayor and captain-general positions. Often the only religious personnel present, Jesuits frequently ministered to the spiritual needs of the few vecinos outside the missions. According to Jesuit reports, in midcentury the Villa de Españoles in Sinaloa (San Felipe) had only some 200 residents, comprising the bulk of the non-Indian population of all Sinaloa–Sonora. Penurious, greedy, uneducated, and morally degenerate, they had only a bare semblance of the *cabildo,* or town government, no permanent division of labor, and not a single skilled craftsman among them — no shoemaker, barber, or tailor.[61] Jesuit contempt sank even lower for the presidial captain and his twenty-five to thirty soldiers of the Montesclaros Fort on the Fuerte River. Lamenting the death in 1626 of the loyal, single-minded Captain Hurdaide, the missionaries bitterly accused his successor, Pedro de Perea, a far more complex individual, of exploiting the riches of Sinaloa–Sonora for personal gains.[62]

Spaniards, civilian and military alike, were interested primarily in two related areas of pursuit: mining and trade. In the first half of the seventeenth century, mining was not yet a well-developed activity. Jesuits reckoned no mines at all in Sinaloa, four or five rather poor ones in Sonora, with only one, the Real de Minas de San Pedro, of any significance.[63] Equally underdeveloped and involving basically foodstuff for the reales, Spanish commerce was also a limited activity. Because vecinos had little agriculture of their own—having only "four small haciendas" in all Sinaloa, according again to the Jesuits—they had to depend on the missions for the basics of survival.[64] This trade exposed the hard-pressed Spaniards all the more to the surplus wealth of the flourishing missions, magnifying in addition Spanish poverty and retarded development.

Resentment added to envy when Spaniards were forced to deal only with missionaries, who prevented them from making direct contacts with the actual Indian producers. In denying constant accusations that Jesuits sold mission goods to enrich themselves, one missionary explained what trade meant to them:

> If one wishes to describe as trade the fact that we took the surplus of our field produce and animals to the Sonoran dwellings of the Spanish miners and sent to the City of Mexico the gold and silver received to buy goods needed by us and by the Indians, I must admit that we did engage in trade.[65]

Later in the seventeenth century, dispute over Jesuit trade would increase in intensity and bitterness.

As long as Spaniards freely expressed their hostile sentiments, Jesuits had their share of complaints. They charged miners and vecinos with exploiting Indians for unpaid personal services and cultivation of food, causing consequently the depopulation of some missions. This seemed a rather exaggerated charge for the moment, for, as the Jesuits themselves revealed, there was only a small number of Spaniards in Sinaloa– Sonora. Their few miserable haciendas and insignificant mines could hardly have necessitated large-scale exploitation of Indian labor and services. However, these early allegations were premonitions of more serious and valid concerns later on.

One real source of worry for Jesuits in midseventeenth century was the voluntary migration of a small but noticeable number of mission Indians from Sinaloa–Sonora to large, established reales de minas of Parral, Chihuahua, Zacatecas, and even, incredibly enough, "New Spain and Guatemala."[66] As early as 1645, if not earlier, some Yaquis had begun leaving their pueblos for the Sierra Madre mines. Pérez de Ribas noted that Yaquis had developed two new material loves soon after Europeans had made contact with them: horses and Spanish clothing and accoutrements, such as the sword. "They would leave the villages and seek work fifty or more leagues out of the province, leaving wife and children behind," using the wages to buy the objects of their newly acquired tastes.[67] Jesuits discredited the migration with the charge that at the reales Indians reverted to their former "savage" existence under the corrupt influence of Spaniards; to be sure, the camps flaunted a more freewheeling and individual life style in contrast to the strict codes and regulated, communal routines of the missions. Still, the early migration had two characteristics that seemed to have kept it within reasonable bounds: it was not of great numerical proportion, and Yaquis left without their families, indicating that their departure was not final or permanent.

While Jesuits began to worry about Yaqui mobility, Spaniards in Nueva Vizcaya had initiated lobbying efforts with the Crown to secularize the missions, that is, to free the Indians legally and effectively from the missionaries' paternalistic tutelage and protection. The bishop of Durango actively supported this movement, for the replacement of missionaries by secular priests, the conversion of missions into parishes, the subjection of Indians to tithes and other taxes, all would have enlarged his jurisdiction. Miners and hacendados would then be able to contract free Indian laborers from the parishes.

In April 1637, the bishop presented to the Crown a petition to secularize the missions of Sinaloa. Even though Sinaloa had no mines, its mission population was considered a valuable source of labor for the Vizcaya mines. The petition painted a picture of prosperity in the Jesuit domain to argue its position that, with such economic progress, surely the mission Indians ought to be ready for tax assessments.[68] The Jesuit provincial in Mexico City—none other than Pérez de Ribas—headed a team of eminent fathers who issued on 12 September 1638 a sharp rebuttal to the bishop's petition. In it they denied all allegations of wealth and success in the Sinaloa missions, and refuted all charges that Jesuits exploited Indians for the benefit of the order. Not surprisingly, they firmly advised against secularization.[69]

To strengthen their argument, Jesuits brandished the much-feared possibility of massive Indian uprisings. They contended that, while the Crown received no direct benefits from the missions in the form of tribute payments, missions pacified Indians and hence ensured the security of the mines. But if these Indians should "rise up, it would be impossible to work [the mines] and obtain any products from them."[70] The argument was logical enough up to this point, but not quite complete. Spaniards would have carried it further: if the pacified Indians could also be induced to work for them cheaply, production from the mines would be even larger, and benefits accruing to the Crown correspondingly more. In their minds, of course, the sole and original purpose of the mission program was to prepare hostile frontier Indians for labor in the Spanish economy. In their response to the first secularization drive, the combative and quick-witted Jesuits must have discovered how difficult it was sometimes to defend their position.

In yet another place in the same rebuttal, Pérez de Ribas and colleagues advanced further unconvincing arguments. On the one hand, they wanted to boast of their apostolic successes in missionizing the indomitable Indians of the northwest in order to justify their continual operation there; on the other hand, they hesitated to emphasize the impressive social and economic gains they had achieved in some of the missions for fear of corroborating the prosecularization position. For this reason, it seemed, they carefully excluded the prosperous Yaqui mission from their lengthy discourse on the miserable conditions of the Sinaloa missions. Yet by 1638, the Yaqui mission was most certainly a well-established fact and had always been considered the northern boundary of Sinaloa province. Three of the coauthors of the document—Andrés Pérez de Ribas, Juan Angelo Balestra, and Juan de Ardeñas—had served as missionaries in the Yaqui. As they could hardly be ignorant of conditions in the Yaqui, its omission from the report must have been intentional. On another occasion around the same time as this report, a less guarded Pérez de Ribas noted proudly that Yaquis worked hard and fared well, producing "in good years ... such an abundance that Spaniards and other Indians could trade with [them]."[71]

Despite difficulties in argument in this initial debate, Jesuits won a de facto victory, for the Crown failed to act on the bishop's petition. This did not put an end to an increasingly heated controversy. In 1657, in response to harsh accusations brought by vecinos in Sinaloa–Sonora, Jesuits felt compelled to issue another lengthy statement in defense of their activities and policies in these provinces. Like the earlier document, this too contained inconsistencies and must be examined with similar caution. It reiterated the missionaries' dedication and hardships while minimizing the growing prosperity of the missions. But the Jesuits could not disguise totally the superior well-being of the missions relative to the floundering existence of the Spanish colonists.[72] This document also provided much additional information about general conditions in the northwest.

As early as 1666, Spaniards began to experience an upturn in their fortunes. They struck a series of mineral deposits in northern Sinaloa: Santa Bárbara, Banachare, Santiago de Tuape, San Francisco del Yaqui, and San Miguel. Two years later, the discovery of Los Gentiles, also known as San Ignacio de Ostimuri y San Marcos, boosted the area between the Yaqui and Mayo rivers into a mining center of some importance. Soon the names of San Ildefonso, San Nicolás, San Francisco de Asís, San Ignacio, Tacupeto, and Bocanora joined the growing roster of mines.[73] In recognition of the newfound significance of northern Sinaloa from the Mayo to the Yaqui rivers inclusive, Governor Oca Sarmiento of Nueva Vizcaya created in October 1668 a new administrative unit, the *alcaldía mayor* or province of San Ildefonso de Ostimuri, taking its name from two reales. More often than not, however, Ostimuri continued to be considered as the northern portion of Sinaloa, rather than as a province in itself.

From 1683 to 1684, Spanish fortunes escalated further as miners discovered a second cluster of rich veins in Ostimuri, in the Cerro de Nuestra Señora de la Concepción de los Frailes near the Mayo River. Better known by its shorter name of Los Alamos, this real was lucratively exploited until well into the eighteenth century. In 1686, Alcalde Mayor Domingo Tuan founded another mining center between Conicari and Camoa on the Mayo River; the Nuestra Señora de Guadalupe y Santo Tomás de Paredes was short-lived, but most productive.[74] Additional mines were also being discovered in Sonora about this time. A few years prior to the discovery of Ostimuri, San Juan Bautista in Sonora was already being worked. According to common practice, this important real served as the capital of the province.[75]

These newly struck mines guaranteed the growth and prosperity of Spanish society, ushering in profound changes which missionaries would find most painful. As long as Yaquis and other Indians had to travel great distances to work mines on the other side of the Sierra Madre, Jesuits did not worry about losing too many of them. And as long as most Spaniards were located far away, they did not have to combat their noxious influence too close to the missions. The bitter experience of the 1616 Tepehuan and other early rebellions had amply demonstrated to them the frustration and futility of attempting to build stable missions in the midst of mining booms.

Much to their distress, then, towards the end of the seventeenth century Jesuits witnessed the emergence in Sinaloa—Sonora of a situation which they had come to deplore in the northeast, with its numerous lucrative mines, its history of devastating Indian rebellions, and its pockets of indigenous communities successfully resisting missionization, such as the mountain Tarahumaras. The famous Parral and other northeastern reales contracted free Indian laborers from all over New Spain. Although they traded with the missions in Sinaloa and Sonora, these reales depended primarily on Spanish grain and stock farms which had sprung up around them to supply their daily subsistence and operational needs.[76]

Sonora and Sinaloa evolved differently. Well before the discovery of significant mines, Jesuits had successfully organized missions wherever they had reached. To the newly arrived miner in the northwest, these pueblos represented the most ready source of available labor and provisions. Spaniards soon learned, however, that while the missionary fathers were quite willing to deal with them commercially, they were totally opposed to releasing their Indian wards as mine workers.

Judging by mounting charges and countercharges that Jesuits and vecinos hurled at each other, the issues of Indian labor and production in the northwest had escalated into a major crisis by 1672. The dispute in that year centered around the question of the legal utilization of Indian labor: who should have access to it and how should Indian workers be remunerated. Among those singled out for special attention were the Yaquis of Ostimuri, the important new mining zone. Both adversaries sharpened their familiar arguments. Miners reasoned that they should be allowed a repartimiento or quota of Indian workers, since missionaries utilized Indian labor in the missions for a variety of purposes without paying them wages. Jesuits, of course, did not see the question of Indian labor in the same way. They maintained that Indians voluntarily worked in the missions towards their own well-being, not for the benefit of any outsiders.[77] When both parties appealed to civil authorities for a ruling, Governor Oca Sarmiento sounded deliberately ambiguous, as if he did not wish to become involved. While he agreed with vecinos that the laws specifically prohibited forced Indian labor without remuneration, he decreed at the same time that no Indian could leave his mission field before it was tilled.[78] The unenforceable ruling added up to another de facto victory for Jesuits; the status quo remained unchanged.

Pursuing their case further, Spaniards finally brought it before the Audiencia of Guadalajara for adjudication. At first Jesuits had smugly expected Francisco de Luque, "Protector of Indians," to represent their interests competently and passionately. To their utter shock and dismay, they heard Luque issue instead a most unflattering, incriminating indictment of mission operations and relationships. According to this testimony, missionaries forced their Indians to plant large fields of maize, beans, and cotton, to perform all the necessary tasks in the pueblos, to work otherwise as slaves. Moreover, they inflicted harsh corporal punishments on those who did not perform their duties satisfactorily and imposed upon the mission communities their own handpicked officials, usually strangers from the outside. Luque further accused the Jesuits of being interested only in advancing their institutional goals, neglecting completely the spiritual commitments of their ministry. Consequently, Luque maintained, Indians begged to pay tribute — to become secularized — in order to be free of the absolutist Jesuit control. He added that the situation in Sonora was far worse than in Sinaloa, for its desolation permitted the powerful fathers to be even more oppressive.[79]

The judge who heard the case, Fernando de Haro y Monterrosos, wrote a long and thoughtful decision. First of all, he decreed that all Indians who worked for others must be paid two-and-a-half *reales* (coins) per day and ordered the freeing of all Indians currently under forced labor.[80] He accompanied these instructions with a strongly worded assessment of mission labor:

> [The Jesuits] are many, and extremely numerous are the Indians they have as subjects, and all the missionaries ... under pretext that the Indians are incapable, make them work, in the fields, in the ranches and in the factories and in any other services, without paying them the daily wage, but handed out rations as if they were mere servants. And although some of these missionaries spend the fruits of this labor on the Indians themselves and on the divine cult, most of them use the profits towards goals completely separated from the missions ... [this despite] the several cédulas granting liberty to the Indians and prohibiting their personal services....[81]

Quite clearly the judge had accepted many of the anti-Jesuit arguments, particularly those directed at Jesuit paternalism and greed.

To the already stunned Jesuits, the judge went on to clarify the boundaries of their legal jurisdiction within the mission. Missionaries were not to inflict corporal punishment on Indians, for this was properly the duty of civil authorities. Nor were they to dispose of produce from the community endeavors, for these rightfully belonged to the Indians themselves, to use as they saw best for their benefits alone. He ended by reminding the fathers that royal decrees specifically prohibited religious personnel from handling temporal affairs.

Jesuits naturally resented this sudden injunction on their supervision of essentially the economic activities of the mission, which threatened to undermine the basis of their hegemony. Retaliating against the harsh words with action, they attempted to demonstrate to the judge far away in Guadalajara how insensitive he was to local conditions. First, they withheld the customary remission of food supplies to the Ostimuri mines, with a pointed query to the alcalde mayor if Spaniards could survive without such provisions. Then, without waiting for the alcalde's response, they produced twenty vecinos from San Miguel de Ostimuri to testify to the indispensability of mission aid to the reales.[82] The purpose of this little scene clearly was to expose the Spaniards' critical dependence on the missions, whose very productivity was made possible by the disputed Indian labor under astute Jesuit management.

Actually, Jesuits need not have resorted to such unsubtle ploys to win out in the end. As in the past, their adversaries, unable to act in concert and enforce their rulings, handed the missionaries another de facto victory. In late 1673 the Audiencia appointed a vecino, Juan Franco Maldonado, to promulgate and implement new decrees terminating nonvoluntary and unpaid labor in the missions. It also charged Alcalde Mayor Miguel Calderón of Sinaloa to investigate the conditions in the missions. What ensued in the Yaqui, where efforts to remove unpaid labor were ultimately ineffectual, was probably typical of what happened elsewhere. According to Maldonado's report, in November 1673, Don Gaspar de Valdés, priest and vicar of the reales of San Juan and San Miguel, and Juan de Encinas, Protector of Indians in Sonora, ordered the Yaqui people to stop serving their missionaries unless they were properly paid. Whereupon the Yaquis became quite excited, began slaughtering mission cattle and demanding the immediate arrival of secular priests. Maldonado felt obligated to rush to the Yaqui and calm the people down, making them understand their duties to their missionaries. Next he proceeded to the Villa de Sinaloa, site of the Jesuit headquarters for the northwest missions, where Indian officials from many pueblos had gathered some Indians into making defamatory remarks against the fathers. and that their resident fathers had not deprived them of their liberty contrary to what had been alleged. Concluding his report to the Audiencia, Maldonado accused Calderón, the "arch-enemy" of the Jesuits, of having sown the seeds of discord in the missions and of having coerced some Indians into making defamatory remarks against the fathers After all, Maldonado noted sarcastically, the alcalde's "bad feelings against the father of the Company of Jesus (which does not surprise me given his official status) is public knowledge."

While Maldonado was carrying out his commission, Alcalde Mayor Calderón had begun freeing some Indians performing what he considered forced labor for the missionaries; these included *mayordomos* (stewards), cowherders, goatherders, soapmakers, porters, fiscales, sacristans and catechists, choristers, cooks, and field hands. He also instructed Indians in some missions to elect new officials to replace those whom the missionaries had handpicked and imposed. In his report, he sought to expose Maldonado's ambivalent mind and subsequent contradictory instructions regarding the new laws. According to Calderón, immediately after Maldonado had publicly announced in the Yaqui the orders prohibiting unpaid labor, he reversed himself by exhorting the Indians "to plant for the missionaries all that they [missionaries] wanted, and that they ought to serve them as before." In other words,

Maldonado advised the Yaquis to ignore the decrees he himself had just issued. Calderón also suggested that perhaps the confusion was not entirely Maldonado's fault. The Jesuits, for obvious reasons, could have deliberately mistranslated Maldonado's words to render them ambiguous. In any case, Calderón concluded, contrary to Maldonado's claim of contented mission populations, the Indians desired their freedom, but their missionaries insisted on keeping them in perpetual bondage.

Maldonado's and Calderón's inability to coordinate their actions left unresolved the question of mission labor. The general dispute lingered on, soon taking on yet another touchy subject, that of control over mission land. Although the land legally belonged to the Indians, there was no doubt that in practice, Jesuits exercised the kind of power associated with actual ownership, for they decided on its availability, distribution, and usages. In Feburary 1674, the Audiencia instructed Governor José García de Salcedo of Nueva Vizcaya to supervise the fair distribution of mission lands between Indians and Spanish vecinos in Sinaloa–Sonora. Again, Jesuits vigorously opposed what was an even clearer move towards secularization. Governor Salcedo apparently bowed to their pressure in acknowledging and tacitly accepting de facto Jesuit ownership of mission land. As he explained to his superiors why he did not act as instructed:

> The Company has and possesses land in these provinces with the title of having entered the missionaries of the Company to convert and preach the faith to heathendom by order of His Majesty, and that this act comprises sufficient title to possess the land and fields which they now make use of.[83]

In the long, drawn-out litigation over Indian labor, produce, and land spanning the years 1672 to 1675, Jesuits defeated the forces of secularization, again because drastic reforms designed to undermine the mission system were not implemented. But each successive crisis shed new light on the relationship between Jesuits and Spaniards on the frontier and on the nature of Hapsburg colonial rule on the periphery of the empire.

On the local level, despite the accelerating drive towards secularization, there was still much disagreement among officials and vecinos over the timing and degree of change. Govenor Salcedo and vecino Maldonado, for example, in discharging their duties at best in a perfunctory manner, implicitly invoked the *Obedesco pero no cumplo* (I obey but do not comply) clause unofficially available to all colonial officials;[84] that is, while acknowledging the theoretical infallibility of the Crown and the Audiencia, they questioned the political wisdom of rulings that threatened to weaken the mission system on the frontier at that particular time. Other officials, such as Alcalde Mayor Calderón and Protector of Indians Fernando Luque, allied and identified more closely with the immediate plight of Spanish hacendados and miners desperate for more Indian labor. At the highest level, the Audiencia, which represented the Crown, was adept at interpreting the principles of colonial rule and royal power, but was often unable to appreciate conflicts and exigencies that conditioned local practices and still less able to enforce its own rulings. As for the faltering Hapsburg monarchy, plagued with its own problems of survival on the continent, it simply could not direct much attention to a frontier of secondary importance.

One important outcome of the recurring disputes — with their heated recriminations, lengthy reports, vituperative charges and counter-charges — was the ream of documentation from all involved parties. Put on the defensive, Jesuits had to divulge new information or provide alternative interpretations of their common practices in order to answer or deflect serious criticisms. Their adversaries were particularly anxious to expose aspects of the mission system which Jesuits had always strenuously avoided discussing in public, such as temporal affairs and material conditions of the pueblos.

By the last quarter of the seventeenth century, the northwestern missions had become stable institutions which kept their Indians generally well fed and busy. The missions' high productivity also underlay the strength of the entire Jesuit evangelical enterprise, assuring the order the means of expanding its empire north into the Pimería Alta and Baja California. Without abandoning their vows of personal poverty, the Jesuits' institutional wealth derived not from outright ownership of property, but from their self-delegated roles as administrators and managers of both the Indians' means of production and fruits of production. They organized work schedules and supervised work teams towards the production of surpluses, then prohibited Indians from engaging in direct trade of their excess produce with Spaniards. In controlling the mission economy from production to distribution, Jesuits prevented the rise of an indigenous elite which would otherwise have emerged with surplus production. Indian cultures, such as the Yaqui, remained essentially egalitarian. Outside the missions, Jesuits also preserved their dominant position through their absolute control over the Indian economy.

Spaniards focused precisely on Jesuit management of mission production to explain why they could not seem to advance their own economic interests with equal facility. Hacendados engaged in agriculture and grazing found it nearly impossible to compete with the Jesuits. As one vecino in Ostimuri noted laconically, the always "dependable" missionary traders consistently undersold their Spanish competitors.[85] They blamed Jesuits, not Indians, for their misfortune, sensing that it was Jesuit control of Indian surpluses that made the missionaries so powerful. Spanish merchants also deeply resented the Jesuits for another reason. The fathers, who insisted on receiving only gold and silver for the produce and cattle they sold, bypassed Spanish agents on the frontier to buy directly from their own brokers in Mexico City. In their customary pragmatic way, one Jesuit rationalized the creation of their own, exclusive commercial network in this way:

> We would have had to give a layman a large salary for his trouble, while the brother of our order procured our goods for us free of charge and needed no salary, for he was supported by the college at Mexico. We could be absolutely certain that this Jesuit would not bill us for more than he really paid for the purchased articles.[86]

This explanation also betrayed an innate mistrust of non-Jesuits. With Indians constituting the vast majority of the local population, the Jesuits' commercial self-reliance obviously deprived Spanish traders of their largest group of potential clients. Moreover, the kind of commerce Jesuits engaged in took more out of the local Spanish economy than it put in and did not serve as much of a stimulant to regional growth.

In spite of the obstacles that Jesuits set in their way, Spaniards doggedly pursued their dream of prosperity. It appeared that towards the end of the seventeenth century their patience was finally being rewarded. Between 1675 and 1684, available figures indicated a fairly successful exploitation of the Sonora and Ostimuri mines. These produced 174,154 *marcos de plata,* or half-pounds of silver, which, compared to the 579,700 marcos produced at the legendary Parral, was not entirely disappointing. In fact, during the year 1683/84, production in the northwest increased markedly while that of Parral declined.[87] Moreover, the discovery of the lucrative Los Alamos mine in Sinaloa in 1683 further stimulated the area's economy. That Spaniards were operating these mines at rather high levels indicated that they had access to a considerable labor force, which could only have come from nearby missions, such as the Yaqui and the Mayo.

Although Jesuits had successfully stalled the movement towards secularization in the seventeenth century, they had no similar luck stemming the voluntary migration of Indians to the mines. Two Jesuit censuses of northwestern missions, in 1662 and 1678, the latter conducted by Father *visitador* (visitor) Juan Ortíz Zapata, called attention to the severity of the problem. The following table summarizes the figures for the Yaqui mission.

TABLE 1

Population of the Yaqui Mission, 1662 and 1678

Pueblo	No. of Families	Total Population	
	1678	1662	1678
Bácum	169	600	510
Cócorit	113	300	337
Tórin	354	1,400	1,070
Vícam	423	1,400	1,271
Ráum	1,184	2,500	3,230
Pótam	433	1,000	1,131
	2,676	7,200	7,549

SOURCES: For 1662: "Catálogo de todas las misiones de la provincia de Nueva España de la Compañía de Jesús. Año de 1662." In Francisco Javier Alegre, *Historia de la provincia de la provincia de la Compañía de Jesús de Nueva España,* vol. 3, pp. 353–54 (Rome: Inst. Hist. S.J., 1956). For 1678: Juan Ortíz Zapata, "Relación de las misiones que la Compañía de Jesús tiene en el reino y provincia de la Nueva Vizcaya en la Nueva España, hecha el año de 1678...." In *Documentos para la historia de México,* ser. 4, no. 3, pp. 375–80 (Mexico: Published for Manuel Orozco y Berra, 1907).

NOTE: In both censuses, two pueblos were left out. Belém, originally a Yaqui pueblo, had apparently been completely taken over by Guaymeño Indians. According to Zapata, in 1678 it had 217 families for 654 individuals. For some unexplained reason, the pueblo of Huírivis was not mentioned at all in either report. Either the census takers missed it on both tours, or, more likely, it was somehow completely depopulated and abandoned.

The last known census of the Yaqui mission was in 1625, during which time Jesuits reported 20,450 baptized individuals.[88] Compared to 7,200 and 7,552 for 1662 and 1678 respectively, there was an apparent sharp demographic decline in the resident mission population during the intervening decades. This did not necessarily mean a drop in the total Yaqui population, however. Or at least the phenomenon could not be accounted for by the conventional causes used to explain the demographic disaster of central and southern New Spain. The long isolation of the missionized Indians of the northwest, with its exteremely small community of Spaniards, did not produce the same kind of devastating contact history that sedentary peoples of the viceroyalty's intensely colonized core region experienced. Although missionaries occasionally mentioned the outbreak of certain diseases—Pérez de Ribas singled out *cocoliztles,* or smallpox, as a serious one[89]—neither Jesuit nor secular sources ever reported widespread epidemics destroying any of the missions. The conclusion, then, is that the low figures did not indicate an absolute decrease, but reflected instead drastic fluctuations in the resident mission population. In other words, Yaquis were moving in and out of their pueblos, undoubtedly to and fro from the mines.* This was exactly the situation that Father Zapata encountered and took note of during 1678.

During his tour of the Yaqui mission, Father Zapata stated simply that "... some pueblos are completely ruined and much of the people lost as a result of ... the exit of many of them to the mines." As for the Mayos, he noted briefly that they were "muy andariegos," or great wanderers, and "often absented themselves from the pueblos." He also made clear that he visited these two missions during a time of high absenteeism, that, in fact, the low figures did not represent the total number of living Yaquis and Mayos.

The voluntary migration of Yaquis and Mayos to the mines was not a new development, of course. Earlier missionaries such as Pérez de Ribas had taken note of it, but also observed that most tended to return after a brief sojourn outside. By some of Zapata's other terse remarks, it appeared that Yaquis continued this same pattern of moving back and forth between mission and mine. For example, Zapata reported that, while all Yaquis still spoke primarily their own language, some had become "muy ladino" or hispanicized.[90] As contact with Spaniards inside the mission was practically nonexistent, these acculturated Indians could only have been returnees from the reales.

A more indirect source of support for this speculation on the nature of Yaqui migration was the level of production in the mission, which continued to be high during periods of apparent high mobility. Had the mission's loss of population been a permanent or year-long one, it would be hard to conceive how it could have maintained large surplus productions. Given the proximity of the mines, Yaquis could have taken turns at leaving, that is, migrated rotationally. They could also have worked the mines on a seasonal basis, seeking outside employment during the mission's slack production period.[91]

Although Jesuits did not customarily record the nature and volume of production in the Yaqui mission, certain activities demonstrated that surpluses remained prodigious. In 1683, when northwestern mines were being lucratively exploited, the mission also supplied impressive quantities of grains, fruits, cattle, and other animals for the first secular expedition into Baja California, in which two Jesuit missionaries participated.[92] Shortly afterwards, the famous Father Eusebio Kino gathered provisions

---

*Figures for the Mayo mission demonstrate even better the Indians' mobility. From 16,800 in 1625, the resident population dropped sharply to a mere 2,000 in 1662, then climbed back to 7,807 in 1678. Of course, this analysis of Yaqui and Mayo mobility was made on the assumption that the censuses were fairly accurately taken.

at the Yaqui for his pioneer evangelical *entrada,* or entry, into the Pimería Alta of Upper Sonora. While in the Yaqui, he remarked with much admiration how resident father Diego Márquina was building "a very pretty new church and house, and sustaining with maize many persons who on account of the drought the year before were suffering great hunger."[93] Again, in 1696, when Jesuits organized their own expedition to Baja California, they mobilized much of their resources from the Yaqui and Mayo missions.[94] Subsequently, when the first California missions were established, to ensure and maximize a steady supply of foodstuffs for them, missionaries actually set aside specific sites in the Yaqui to produce solely and exclusively for the new converts, even constructing special granaries and warehouses in designated pueblos. In addition to grains, Yaquis delivered thousands of heads of cattle and sheep from their communal ranches to California.[95]

Even in terms of manpower, Yaquis were able to offer substantial aid to the Jesuits in California. They composed the navigating crews on boats plying between the mouth of the Yaqui River and the peninsular coast.[96] They served as apostolic assistants to the first missionaries and participated as auxiliaries in the exploration of unknown parts of Baja California, such as Father Ugarte's entrada to the southern tip in 1706. In 1735, when Father Bravo appealed to Yaquis for eighty men to help suppress a general rebellion on the peninsula, reportedly 500 Yaquis volunteered.[97] In sum, the Yaquis' timely and generous aid to the California and Pimería Alta missions attested to their mission's vitality, prosperity, and basic stability, even as many of them moved freely and frequently to and from the mines.* The ability to offer this kind of critical assistance also underscored the Jesuit fathers' skillful political and economic management of the Yaqui mission. Both Brigadier Pedro de Rivera, who toured the Ostimuri, Sinaloa, and Sonora presidios from 1724 to 1726, and the bishop of Nueva Vizcaya heaped lavish praise on the Yaquis and their missionaries, even as they deplored the general state of deterioration throughout the north, caused by increasing Apache and other Indian depredations.[98]

---

*There could be other possible explanations to reconcile the concurrent large-scale migration and continuous high mission production. With better technology, decades of experience, and other improvements, conceivably fewer workers were required to maintain or even increase the traditional level of mission production, in which case the large number of absentees might have had little adverse effect. It was also possible that the Yaqui population had grown too numerous for the available land — especially when Jesuits seemed to require more grains and cattle for their own expanded evangelical activities — necessitating a certain amount of migration to release some of the pressure off the land. These are all pure speculations, however, unsupported by any available evidence.

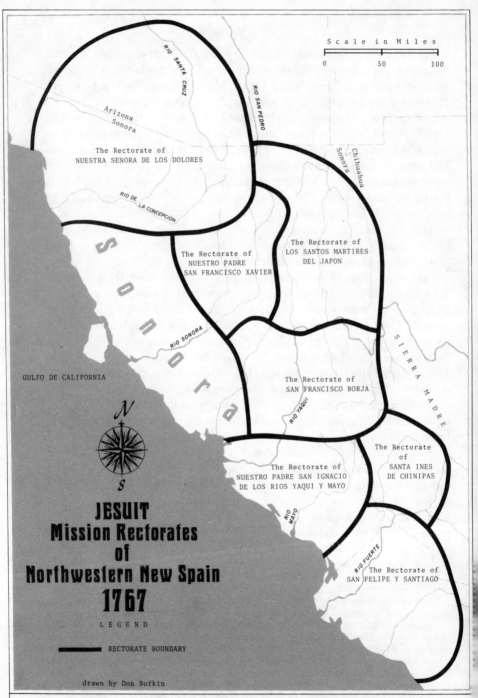

Maps 1A and 1B: Jesuit Missions and Rectorates of Northwestern New Spain, 1767

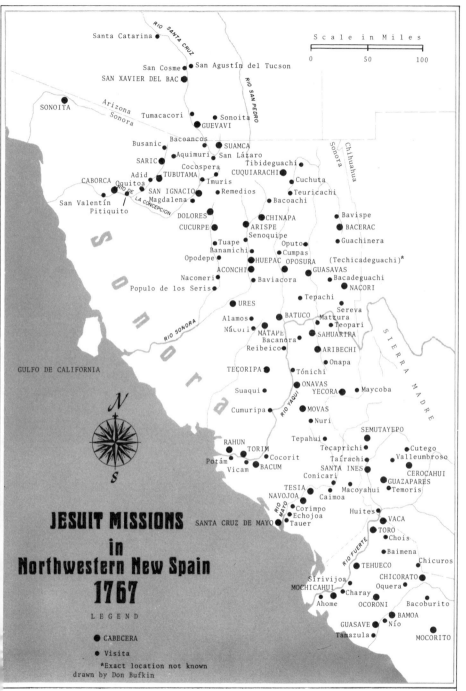

Santa Catarina ●

RIO SANTA CRUZ

Scale in Miles

0   50   100

San Cosme ●● San Agustín del Tucson

SAN XAVIER DEL BAC ●

SONOITA ●

Arizona Sonora

Tumacacori ●

Sonoita ●

RIO SAN PEDRO

GUEVAVI ●

Busanic ●

Bacoancos ●

SUAMCA ●

Chihuahua Sonora

SARIC ●

Aquimuri ●

San Lázaro ●

Tibideguachi ●

Cocóspera ●

CUQUIARACHI ●

Adid ●

TUBUTAMA ●

Imuris ●

Cuchuta ●

CABORCA ●

Oquitoa ●

RIO DE

SAN IGNACIO ●

Remedios ●

Teuricachi ●

San Valentín ●

LA CONCEPCION

Magdalena ●

Bacoachi ●

Pitiquito ●

DOLORES ●

CHINAPA ●

Bavispe ●

CUCURPE ●

ARISPE ●

BACERAC ●

Senoquipe ●

Tuape ●

Oputo ●

Guachinera ●

Banamichi ●

Cumpas ●

Opodepe ●

HUEPAC ●

OPOSURA ●

(Techicadeguachi)*

ACONCHI ●

GUASAVAS ●

Nacomeri ●

Baviacora ●

Bacadeguachi ●

Populo de los Seris ●

NACORI ●

Tepachi ●

URES ●

Sereva ●

Alamos ●

BATUCO ●

Matzura ●

Nácori ●

Teopari ●

MATAPE ●

SAHUARIPA ●

Bacanora ●

Reibeico ●

ARIBECHI ●

Onapa ●

GULFO DE CALIFORNIA

TECORIPA ●

Tónichi ●

ONAVAS ●

Suaqui ●

YECORA ●

Maycoba ●

Cumuripa ●

RIO YAQUI

MOVAS ●

Nuri ●

SEMUTAYEPO ●

Tepahui ●

RAHUN ●

TORIM ●

Tecaprichi ●

Cutego ●

Potám ●

Cocorit ●

Tairachi ●

Valleumbroso ●

Vicam ●

BACUM ●

SANTA INES ●

Conicari ●

CEROCAHUI ●

TESIA ●

GUAZAPARES ●

NAVOJOA ●

Macoyahui ●

Temoris ●

Caimoa ●

JESUIT MISSIONS
in
Northwestern New Spain
1767

SANTA CRUZ DE MAYO ●

RIO MAYO

Corimpo ●

Huites ●

VACA ●

Echojoa ●

Tauer ●

TORO ●

Chois ●

Baimena ●

RIO FUERTE

Chicuros ●

TEHUECO ●

CHICORATO ●

Sirivijoa ●

MOCHICAHUI ●

Oquera ●

Charay ●

Ahome ●

OCORONI ●

Bacoburito ●

LEGEND

BAMOA ●

GUASAVE ●

Nío ●

● CABECERA

Tamazula ●

MOCORITO ●

● Visita

*Exact location not known

drawn by Don Bufkin

From: Charles W. Polzer, *Rules and Precepts of the Jesuit Missions of Northwestern New Spain* (Tucson: University of Arizona Press, 1976).

Beginning around 1680, the ill effects of the accelerated, intensified Spanish – Indian contact of the last several decades erupted into a wave of rebellions that continued into the next century. Apaches, Pueblos, Seris, Tarahumaras, were among the many nations who revolted against missionary and colonial rule.[99] In 1690, rebels from the Pima Bajo pueblo of the northwest set fire to the real of Tacupeto in Ostimuri, arousing grave fears that the contagion of rebellion would spread to the quiescent, industrious Yaqui, Mayo, and Fuerte missions. Captain Diego de Quirós, with fifty vecinos and presidial soldiers and another 150 Yaqui auxiliaries, managed to extinguish the fire and contain the uprising in the eastern half of the province. But in the panic of the moment, old antagonisms which had been momentarily suppressed flared up again as Jesuits and Spaniards blamed each other for the outbreak of the Pima revolt. Captain Quirós accused missionaries of having imposed an unpopular mayordomo on the Pimas, while Jesuits charged Quirós with inept handling of the crisis.[100]

A Jesuit ally appeared to have been the alcalde of Ostimuri, who attributed the main cause of the Pima uprising to:

> ... the damages which [the rebels] received from Spaniards who took away their land and populated it with horses and cattle, and who exacted excessive work from them for two years.... The Indians could no longer cultivate their land because the beasts damaged it and ate the crops.[101]

An all-too-familiar transgression in central New Spain, Spanish encroachment on Indian land was only a recent development in the northwest. Their mission still relatively new and not stabilized sufficiently to withstand strong pressures from the outside, the Pima tragedy reflected the growing Spanish presence on the frontier and presaged an imminent widespread disintegration of order and stability.

At the end of the seventeenth century, the northwest had extended to the Gila River in Arizona, requiring greater administrative attention. In 1734, the Crown detached the five coastal provinces of Rosario, Culiacán, Sinaloa, Ostimuri, and Sonora from Nueva Vizcaya, constituting them into a new political jurisdiction to be known simply as Sinaloa and Sonora.[102] The political reform also forced Jesuits to confront the unpleasant fact that gone forever were the halcyon days of their preeminence and the splendid isolation of the missions. During the next century, they had to compete more vigorously and bitterly than ever before with a growing Spanish society for access to the valuable resources of Indian land and labor.

Also becoming better delineated in the eighteenth century was a key theme of colonial frontier history, the inability of missions and mines as competing institutions to accommodate each other and to coexist in the same environment. Although missions were originally conceived to pacify and acculturate indomitable frontier Indians to serve larger colonial designs, Jesuits had redefined their purposes, which turned out not at all complementary to secular interests. Caught in the middle of Jesuit-Spanish competition were the Yaquis and other mission Indians who constituted, on the one hand, the raison d'etre for the Jesuits' permanent work on the frontier and provided, on the other hand, the motor force for the operation of Spanish mines and haciendas. Initially Yaquis attempted to satisfy both demands; they went to the mines but also upheld the mission system. In 1740, however, Yaquis led a massive uprising that engulfed all of Ostimuri and most of Sinaloa. The pressures had become intolerable.

CHAPTER 4

Exit the Jesuits

In 1767, the Bourbon monarch Charles III unceremoniously expelled the entire Jesuit order from New Spain and the rest of Spanish America, laid claim on the immense wealth Jesuits had allegedly accumulated, and reasserted the Crown as the primary authority over the vast territory Jesuit missionaries had once held sway. In New Spain's northwest, the expulsion did not produce as much widespread disorder as it did in other parts of the empire; it actually culminated an ongoing process of declining Jesuit influence over the Yaqui and other mission populations and within the larger frontier society. Master reformer José de Gálvez considered the drastic measure a necessary first step in his grand design to pacify the rebellious Indians on the frontier and to revitalize the mining economy. The long-neglected colonists and miners of this remote region naturally welcomed the visitor general's farsighted vision and energetic initiatives. While the Crown transferred the recently missionized or still unsubjugated peoples of Sonora to Franciscan missionaries, it intended at the same time to secularize the Jesuit missions of Ostimuri and Sinaloa, that is, to integrate these Indians into the developing Spanish society.

Implicitly, this assimilation would take place at the lowest social level, for the Indians were conceived to be the source of cheap and docile labor.

Yaquis facilitated Gálvez's political and economic reforms in several ways, but also thwarted his other plans for total integration. Long before the visitor general had arrived on the scene, Yaquis had begun asserting their independence from the missionaries, who, after more than a century of peaceful tutelage, still insisted on treating the Yaqui people as immature wards needy of their close protection and constant guidance. The challenge to Jesuit hegemony could be traced back to 1740, year of the first — and only — major Yaqui rebellion while under missionary rule. While not the only revolt to rock the Jesuit empire in the late seventeenth and early eighteenth century, it was one of the most serious, and its leaders unquestionably the most distinctive and articulate about their goals. Following the 1740 uprising, the Yaqui mission itself experienced a new threat, as it assumed a defense posture for the first time against rebellious Seris, Pimas and other Indians who with apparent facility were pushing the unstable frontier line farther and farther south. Both the rebellion and the exigency of defense brought Yaquis into closer contact with colonial military personnel, whose growing presence within the mission broke the resident father's monopoly of authority. Together with accelerated Yaqui migration to the mines after 1740, these experiences permanently weakened Jesuit supremacy, hence significantly softening the impact of their expulsion.

Far from disintegrating, the Yaqui pueblos sans Jesuits maintained a vigorous cultural life and economic self-sufficiency. Furthermore, by accommodating themselves voluntarily as wage laborers to the expanding mining economy outside the mission, they forestalled implementation of other reforms designed for their total integration into secular Spanish society. While many other indigenous nations of the northwest helplessly underwent forced cultural transformation and social breakdown, Yaquis successfully protected their distinct cultural identity and retained a cohesive political unity — both legacies of their long mission experience. And once again, the Yaquis' own characteristic flexibility and ingenuity in meeting new circumstances had served them well. By the time of Mexican Independence in 1821, the Yaqui people had learned to survive on their own terms, premised on a separatism and autonomy that did not necessarily entail total isolation from the rest of society.

The Rebellion of 1740

The acrimonious exchanges between Jesuits and secular Spaniards in the seventeenth century climaxed in a wave of rebellions in the eighteenth century that in turn signalled the decline of Jesuit hegemony in the northwest. Missions and mines developed into competing, ultimately irreconcilably antagonistic institutions, for both depended on scarce Indian labor and resources for survival and growth. The proud self-sufficiency and expansionist tendencies of the mission system proved incompatible with the more interdependent and integrated society and economy that Spaniards strove to foster in the same environment.

Three interrelated issues of the Jesuit–Spanish power struggle came to a head to produce the 1740 Yaqui rebellion and others that followed. In the first place, as their prospects for development brightened, miners and hacendados intensified pressures for more Indian produce and especially labor. Second, local civil and military authorities more forcefully asserted their rightful jurisdiction over temporal affairs in the missions. Finally, Indians themselves began for the first time to express desires for certain fundamental changes in the mission system. Faced with these challenges all at once, the Jesuit fathers responded not so much with sensitive flexibility as with a tough defensiveness that with time and frustration eventually settled into resignation.

In the colonial history of the northwest, the 1740 Yaqui rebellion was one of the outstanding events. Not only did it erupt in the region's most successful and prosperous mission, but it posed a monumental threat when the Yaqui rebels inspired a large following among the mission peoples of the other three great rivers of the province: the Mayo, the Fuerte, and the Sinaloa. With only the Pimas Altos of Sonora uninvolved in any significant way, the rebellion which came to include just about every indigenous nation of the northwest presented to many Spaniards the frightening spector of a race war bent on annihilating the small white population and hence colonial rule.

While its magnitude caused deep concern, the origin and course of its pacification raised the most heated and intense discussions. Among those who had a stake in its outcome, there was little agreement on the crucial questions: what caused the outbreak, how best to resolve the conflict, who were the actual rebel leaders, and what were their motivations? Most bitterly disputed perhaps was the question of who provoked or encouraged the Yaquis to rise up: Governor Manuel Bernal de Huidobro and his "bad government" or Jesuit missionaries and their intolerably authoritarian and arbitrary rule? Huidobro, whom Viceroy Duque de la Conquista removed from office in January 1741, could only regain his honor and office by proving Jesuit guilt. Morally devastated by the rebellion, Jesuits absolved themselves of all blame by turning the full force of their argument and influence against the governor, with his well-known prosecularization sentiments. To mediate the charges and countercharges, high officials from viceroys and their advisors to the

Council of Indies and the Crown in Spain scrupulously and repeatedly examined every piece of data concerning this controversial rebellion. The lengthy investigation, not concluded until 1744, produced a ream of documentation[1] from which the following events and relationships emerge as significant factors.

The gradual buildup of tension in the Yaqui mission and vicinity could be traced to a series of conflicts beginning in 1735. In September of that year, Pedro Álvarez Acevedo, militia captain, vecino, and minero of the Real of San Francisco Asís in the town of Río Chico, complained to local authorities that he had to suspend all work in his mines for lack of *operarios,* or laborers. Ostimuri's alcalde mayor, Miguel de Quiroz, ordered Yaqui captain-general Cristóbal de Gurrola and the native magistrates of Pótam to send Acevedo a certain number of men; but his orders went unheeded. In October and November, other Ostimuri miners echoed the same complaint on the critical shortage of mine workers. The year before, they added, they had experienced difficulty recruiting sufficient men from the authorized mission pueblos for the mining season, which ran from October to May. This year, they lamented, the situation had worsened, for "not one peon was to be found," this despite Governor Huidobro's specification of fortnightly rotation, or *tapisque,* of twenty men each turn.

When Yaquis repeatedly ignored the vecinos' solicitations, some of them charged Father Diego González of Pótam with advising his Indians to defy deliberately the Crown's officials. According to vecino José Ignacio Valenzuela, the father counseled his Yaquis not to consider themselves the Spaniards' *topiles,* or servants, and even dictated for them a written refusal to comply with the call for tapisques.[2] On December 11, an exasperated Alcalde Quiroz lashed out at the Jesuits in a letter to the governor, then conducting an Indian campaign in Baja California. Quiroz bluntly accused the padres of being the

> ... cause for the Indians' failure to obey the authorities, because these missionaries so dominated them that they only did what the padres wished, and the padres wanted to be despotic lords, who install and depose gobernadores at their whim ... as if each padre in his station was so absolute that there were no sovereign power than he alone.[3]

Commenting on this conflict at a later date, Jesuits admitted that they intervened to prevent their Indians from going to the mines. But they maintained that they acted justifiably "because they [miners] only paid a ridiculous wage, or with worthless goods." The Jesuits also characterized Acevedo disparagingly as a *miserable* who found it easier "to deceive the Yaquis than to deceive children." Moreover, they continued, Yaquis did not want to obey Alcalde Quiroz out of concern for their own health, hence their reluctance to travel the sixty-league distance to Acevedo's mines.[4]

Not resting with this response, Jesuits counterattacked by relating a story of their own, also dated around 1735. They accused Don Andrés de Quiroz, brother of Miguel de Quiroz, of coveting a piece of land in the Tepahui mission adjacent to the Yaqui. The Indians resisted his attempted encroachment "because they did not want Spaniards to live among them." Tepahui's resident father Patricio Imaz then escorted both parties to see Padre Visitador Pedro Reinaldo to resolve the dispute in a "just and friendly way." Together Fathers González, Imaz, and Reinaldo, "in view of the justness" of the Indians' position, deterred Quiroz from pressing his claim. But when Governor Huidobro appointed Don Andrés's brother, Don Miguel, as alcalde mayor of Ostimuri, the missionaries interpreted the act as retaliation for the intervention in the Tepahui dispute. According to them, the two Quiroz brothers "liberally offered Indian land to Spaniards," causing enormous pain that began to plunge the Indians "into desperation." Huidobro himself was no better, for he also measured off land in the Yaqui mission and encouraged the people to demand *clérigos,* or priests, to replace the Jesuit fathers. It was the Spanish usurpation of Indian land that led to the outbreak of rebellion in 1740, the fathers concluded in an authoritative tone that suggested no further discussion necessary.[5]

While the battle line was being drawn between Jesuits on the one hand and the governor and certain vecinos on the other, another source of conflict appeared. In March 1736, Yaqui militia captain and gobernador of Ráum pueblo, Juan Ignacio Usacamea, better known as El Muni, led a group of unhappy Yaquis to see Alcalde Quiroz. Several recent occurrences in the mission, which had nothing directly to do with the vecinos' labor plight or with Spanish land grabs, troubled them deeply. First, they expressed dissatisfaction with their captain-general, Cristóbal de Gurrola, for treating his people cruelly and unfairly. The highest of the presumably elected native magistrates, Gurrola was most likely handpicked and imposed by the missionaries according to established practice. Throughout the turmoil of 1740, he remained unpopular with his own people and consistently loyal to the padres.

Muni and companions appeared even more agitated about a small but highly visible and vocal group of outsiders then residing in their pueblos. Derogatorily labeled *coyotes* by the Yaquis, these were mestizos, mulattoes, other mixed bloods, or even Indians of other nations whom the Jesuits had installed in positions of trust and confidence within the mission. The coyote Juan Frías, for instance, was Father Diego González's fiscal at Huírivis.* Already resentful of the coyotes' elevated status, the Yaquis accused this abusive, greedy lot of oppressing Yaquis in numerous ways, including extortion, land usurpation, and conspiracy to turn their padres against them. To illustrate the point, Muni related a personally galling incident that was also typical of coyote behavior. Coyote Juan Frías accused Muni of stealing Father González's storehouse keys with intention of breaking into it. When another Yaqui refused to whip Muni at Frías's direction, the coyote had them both punished. Then it was discovered that the son of another coyote had actually lost the keys. Frías offered no apologies or compensation for the false accusation and unwarranted punishment.

In the wake of Muni's bold example, other disgruntled Yaquis also sought out Alcalde Quiroz with similar complaints. As for Muni himself, although he had carefully avoided implicating the missionaries directly, his unprecedented initiative had marked him out as a troublemaker in Jesuit and coyote eyes. Not long after his visit to Quiroz, coyote Ignacio Alipazaga, nicknamed *El Barrigón* (Big Belly), ordered Muni's arrest on grounds of attempting to foment an uprising. The gobernador of Huírivis, Bernabé Basoritemea, who was Muni's *compadre* and closest collaborator, reiterated to Quiroz the growing conviction among many Yaquis that the coyotes were the real agitators and troublemakers in their communities.

Again the Jesuits counteracted, this time by sending a large contingent of loyal Yaquis to visit Quiroz. Led by Captain-General Gurrola and accompanied by Father José Roldán, these Yaquis declared that they all lived in peace and harmony in the mission, with nothing to complain about. Far from discrediting the dissidents, this gesture was not particularly persuasive to a local official who was clearly not a Jesuit friend or ally. In any case, Quiroz's term expired in the midst of this mounting controversy. His lackluster successor, Francisco Ordóñez, tried with little success to placate the Yaquis and mollify the Jesuits.

The next official who stepped into the case fared no better; in fact, he actually caused a major crisis. In October, with no resolution in sight and the govenor still absent, Lieutenant Governor Manuel de Mena felt compelled to intervene. First, he sent word to Muni and Bernabé, who were on their way to see him at the provincial capital Sinaloa, to return home and wait for him there. Once at the Yaqui, however, instead of taking

---

*Gonzáles was resident father of the pueblos of Ráum and Huírivis, whose gobernadores in 1736 were, respectively, Muni and Bernabé Basoritemea, Muni's close companion and collaborator.

testimony from all sides and mediating the discord with justice, as he had promised the Yaquis, Mena acted with undue haste and allowed himself to be easily swayed by the eloquent Jesuits. After Fathers Pedro Reinaldo, Diego González, Ignacio Duque, and Bartolomé Fentanes had plied him with rich foods, lavish gifts, and high praises, Mena ordered the arrest of Muni, Bernabé, and other dissident Yaquis, as well as former Alcalde Mayor Miguel de Quiroz. When a group of vecinos attempted to disabuse him of the notion that these Yaquis were fomenting an uprising, the lieutenant governor brushed them aside. In no way did the missionaries and their newfound ally anticipate the swift and volatile reaction of the Yaqui people to the sudden arrests. In front of the community house-turned-jail at Pótam, Muni's nephew and confidant, Luis Aquibuamea, led an awesome crowd of irate Yaquis, estimated at 2,000 and armed with bows and arrows, to demand the immediate release of their imprisoned brothers. Having only a small armed escort with him, the intimidated Mena capitulated. At his request, Muni calmed down and dispersed his supporters; then he and his companions were released.

The Pótam incident deeply embarrassed the lieutenant governor and seriously compromised his authority in the eyes of all Indians in the province. In fact, his humiliation caused all white men, vecinos and Jesuits alike, to suffer loss of prestige and honor. Conversely, the aura surrounding the Yaquis' large and spontaneous demonstration greatly enhanced the self-esteem and confidence of all Indians, at the same time bolstering Muni and Bernabé's reputation and popularity throughout the province. Perhaps to save face, Mena kept Quiroz prisoner and remitted him to Guadalajara for judgment. He himself was soon relieved of office.

Among the first to inform Mexico of the ill-fated Mena visit were those vecinos whom the lieutenant governor had rudely ignored. In November 1736, fifteen of them signed a collective letter to Juan Antonio de Vizarrón y Eguiarreta, commonly known as the "archbishop-viceroy" because he held both positions. They gave a terse account of Mena's mishandling of the Yaqui crisis, emphasizing his adamant refusal to take their testimony while falling easy prey to the Jesuits' sweet words and generosity. These vecinos also took the opportunity to bring up again the issue of labor shortage, which had remained unresolved. Because Jesuits exploited Yaquis to reap yearly profits of 2,000 to 3,000 pesos per year, they argued, the Indians desired to be freed of Jesuit tutelage and to pay tribute to the Crown, in short, to be secularized. In view of these sentiments, they continued, the Pótam fiasco was especially lamentable because Mena had damaged the Crown's credibility just when Yaquis and other Indians were ready to become mature, tax-paying subjects.

When the viceroy responded to the vecino's letter and to other reports on the same incident, he skirted entirely the issues of labor shortage and secularization, concerning himself only with the demonstration itself. Pardoning all those Yaquis who had rebelled against Mena, Vizarrón invited their leaders to write or see him personally in Mexico about their grievances. He also ordered the release of Quiroz. The judgment was clearly against Mena, and, by association, the Jesuits as well. Its impact was delayed, however, for the letter, dated in March 1737, did not arrive in Sinaloa until May 1738, over a year late. In the meantime, the relationship between missionaries and Yaquis deteriorated further.

Lieutenant Governor Mena was not the only political casualty in the immediate aftermath of Pótam. As if acknowledging their own difficulties in managing Yaqui affairs, Fathers Diego González and Ignacio Duque asked to be relieved of their posts. Unfortunately, their successor, Father Ignacio María Nápoli, a transfer from Baja California, failed to heal the wounds as next resident father of Pótam, Ráum, and Huírivis. In fact, during the next three years, many of Father Nápoli's actions and policies intensified the hostility and mistrust that were already dividing the troubled mission. With increasing regularity, Muni and Bernabé defied the authority of the father and his Yaqui and coyote assistants.

Immediately upon taking charge in November 1736, Nápoli felt it necessary to assert his authority over Muni and Bernabé, still gobernadores of Ráum and Huírivis, respectively. He ordered Bernabé to punish several Indians of Huírivis suspected of stealing goods destined for California. Bernabé refused on grounds that he did not believe the accused to be guilty. After a series of similar unpleasant confrontations, Muni and Bernabé were suddenly out of their offices. Nápoli claimed that the two had resigned. But Bernabé informed the new lieutenant governor, Cayetano Fernández de Peralta, that the missionary had peremptorily ousted him and Muni. Whereupon Peralta dispatched a special emissary, the vecino Don Manuel Gaspar de Flores of Baroyeca, to reinstate Muni and Bernabé. He also took care to write the Jesuit vicerector of Sinaloa, Father Andrés García, to protest his loyalty to the order. Emissary Flores did not find his task easy to carry out. At the Yaqui, the loyal Captain-General Gurrola assured him that all Yaquis were happy with Father Nápoli. Yet a perceptive Flores detected signs of widespread support for Muni and Bernabé. For example, he noted that at the mass said for the new gobernador of Ráum—handpicked by Nápoli—few men, and mostly women, attended. The cautious Spaniard decided to suspend his orders, instructing Muni and Bernabé instead to see Peralta personally in Sinaloa.

Escorted by thirty valorous, armed and mounted men, Muni and Bernabé arrived at the provincial capital flexing their muscles. Peralta found himself in a most difficult bind: how to placate the angry Yaquis without further alienating the sensitive Jesuits, who threatened to excommunicate him if he made the wrong move. In February 1738, he succeeded in persuading the Yaquis to return to their pueblos. Somehow he had also talked Muni and Bernabé into apologizing to Father Nápoli, who promptly declared himself skeptical of the Yaquis' sincerity.

In July 1738, Governor Huidobro finally returned from Baja California, where he had squabbled bitterly with the missionaries. He proceeded immediately to the Yaqui mission to verify for himself the numerous and often conflicting reports he had been receiving. At Pótam, Gurrola and the gobernadores of Ráum, Huírivis, and Pótam—Nápoli's pueblos—delivered to him separate written complaints against Muni, Bernabé, and seventeen others. These statements charged the dissidents with insubordination and rebelliousness, that is, encouraging other Yaquis to follow their leadership instead of obeying the fathers. In addition, they accused Muni of plotting to make himself captain-general and Bernabé perpetual gobernador of Huírivis.

When Huidobro interrogated the gobernadores on the spot, he heard oral testimonies that contradicted the written statements. The native magistrates revealed that they were actually in complete ignorance of the contents of their formal presentations, which Father Nápoli had handed to them for delivery to the governor. It turned out that the padre's coyote assistants, Juan María Alcalá and Ignacio Alipazaga, had penned the indictments according to Nápoli's instructions. Discovery of this deception did not appear to have embarrassed Father Nápoli, however. He merely went before Huidobro himself to repeat with even greater vehemence the same denunciations. Ever since these disloyal Yaquis went unpunished for taking up arms against Mena, he fumed, they had become increasingly insolent, losing all respect not only for the missionaries, but for all Spaniards as well. Moreover, Muni and Bernabé had appropriated all communal goods in their publos for themselves, leaving nothing for the padres. Many Yaquis were already worshipping Muni on their knees as if he were God, Nápoli warned; he was convinced that the Devil had possessed Muni. In closing, the father characterized Muni and Bernabe's irreverent behavior as *hombrearse*, presuming to act like Spaniards. They called themselves "Señor gobernador" and "Señor Muni," went everywhere with an armed retinue complete with flags and military insignias, and otherwise dressed like Spaniards, with guns, swords, and all.

Never having been partial to Jesuits in the first place, Huidobro explained it was only fair to give the Yaquis an open hearing as well. On

22 July, before a large gathering of Indians in Pótam plaza, Muni and Bernabé recited to the governor their familiar litany of outstanding complaints against Gurrola and the padres' abusive coyote assistants. In addition, they expressed unhappiness about the excessive workloads the missionaries demanded of them, their wives, and children, especially for labor related to the production and transportation of goods and cattle for the California missions. Their communal ranches were impoverished because the fathers had just dispatched 500 to 600 heads of cattle to the peninsula and sold 200 heads each to Los Alamos and to Villa de Sinaloa for silver. Yet the Yaqui people did not see or enjoy the profits from the sale of their mission surpluses. The padres also expropriated the sweat of Yaqui labor when they presented the expensive gifts to Lieutenant Governor Mena in 1736. Finally, the Pótam gathering vented resentment at the harsh corporal punishments they often suffered, frequently for little or no cause.

At the end of this emotion-packed public hearing, Governor Huidobro heightened the excitement by reading aloud Archbishop-Viceroy Vizarrón's letter of March 1737, which had conveniently just arrived. The missive which exonerated Yaquis for their armed confrontation with Mena and invited their leaders for a private audience in Mexico left them feeling vindicated. In October, encouraged by Huidobro's blessing, Muni and Bernabé set off for the colonial capital; they would not return until late in 1740, when the rebellion was in its final moments. The governor's last act before departing the Yaqui was to hold new elections in Pótam, Huírivis, and Ráum to replace the unpopular gobernadores whom Father Nápoli had imposed.

If Huidobro's actions went far to placate the Yaqui dissidents, they had the opposite effect on the missionaries, who seriously questioned the governor's wisdom in publicizing Vizarrón's condemnation of Mena and in encouraging Muni and Bernabé to accept the viceroy's invitation. Not surprisingly, they interpreted Huidobro's behavior as hostile to Jesuit interest and an incitement to rebellion. Throughout 1738 and 1739, they kept alerting local authorities to disturbances in the Yaqui, such as armed individuals in war paints arresting Indians loyal to the padres and threats made on missionary lives. To their despair and exasperation, Huidobro and Alcalde Mayor José de Acedo y Bea of Ostimuri dismissed these notices as "false alarms" not worthy of attention. By this time, missionaries were inclined to call any act of insubordination a sure sign of impending revolt. They even began dismantling mission churches of valuable ornaments and packing them off to California for safekeeping, an act which irate Yaquis would add to their long list of abuses. Also, still pending was the problem of labor shortages for the mines. When pressed, Father Nápoli insisted that he could not spare any Yaquis for the vecinos, but Alcalde Acedo maintained that he saw large numbers of Indians working for the missionaries in various capacities.

While old problems and conflicts remained unresolved, new ones arose during Muni and Bernabé's long absence preceding the outbreak of rebellion in early 1740. Alternating droughts and floods in the Yaqui Valley and vicinity caused the destruction of crops and cattle, leading consequently to severe food shortages and widespread hunger. A totally unfamiliar sight surfaced in this area — that of hungry Yaquis wandering about the sierra foraging for edible materials to sustain themselves. Soon desperate Indians began raiding mission granaries and nearby Spanish haciendas and ranches for food. The resident fathers' handling of the famine departed notably from the tradition that their predecessors had established. Seldom, if ever, under Jesuit rule did Yaquis have to resort to the aboriginal practice of gathering wild foods or to acts of banditry for survival; missionaries had always managed to take adequate care of the hungry masses from the stored supplies in the pueblos. This time, however, in 1739, they announced that they were reserving the bulk of the surplus provisions for the California missions, an insensitive decision that some Yaquis could only interpret as vindictiveness. When other Indians in the flood-damaged region approached the prosperous Yaqui mission for relief, they were turned away empty-handed. Allegedly, when Nápoli finally relented to sell a niggardly amount of maize, he demanded an exorbitant price.[6] The faithful coyote Juan Frías gave his eyewitness testimony on the crisis in this way:

> ... I heard say that the motive for the uprising in the beginning was none other than that the river had swelled a lot, destroying all the cattle and crops of Bácum, that because of this they [Yaquis] fled up a hill, that from there they began to plunder; that because Father Fentanes punished them, they became incensed and threw him out of the mission.[7]

In other words, Juan Frías clearly linked the famine with the rebellion.

By February 1740, widespread acts of banditry led directly to the beginnings of a massive, but uncoordinated, often leaderless uprising. Large numbers of Mayos had joined forces with their Yaqui neighbors, plundering and raiding to such alarming proportions that vecinos in more isolated locations began to abandon their mines and homes for more secure, larger towns and haciendas. By April, the Yaqui River was "all drums and arrows;" by the end of May, reportedly groups of Fuerteños, Guaymeños, and other Pima Bajo groups had also risen up, although not to the universal extent that would have justified some alarmist cries of an all-out *guerra de casta,* or race war. From

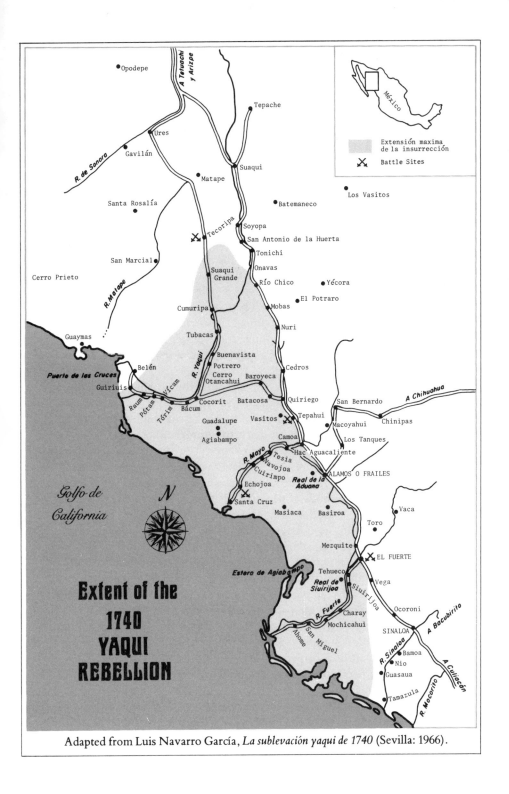

Opodepe

Tepache

Ures

Gavilán

R. de Sonora

Suaqui

Matape

Santa Rosalía

Batemaneco

Los Vasitos

Tecoripa

Soyopa

San Antonio de la Huerta

San Marcial

Tonichi

Suaqui
Grande

Onavas

Cerro Prieto

Río Chico

Yécora

R. Matape

El Potraro

Cumuripa

Mobas

Guaymas

Tubacas

Nuri

Buenavista

Belén

R. Yaqui

Potrero
Cerro
Otancahui

Cedros

Puerto de las Cruces

Baroyeca

Guiriuis

A Chihuahua

Raum

Pótam

Tórim

Yécam

Bácum

Cocorit

Batacosa

Quiriego

San Bernardo

Guadalupe

Vasitos

Tepahui

Chinipas

Agiabampo

Camoa

Macoyahui

Los Tanques

Hac Aguacaliente

R. Mayo

Tesia

Navojoa

Cuirimpo

Real de la
Aduana

ALAMOS O FRAILES

Echojoa

Santa Cruz

Masiaca

Basiroa

Vaca

Golfo de
California

N

Toro

Mezquite

EL FUERTE

Estero de Agiabampo

Tehueco

Real de
Siuirijoa

Vega

Siuirijoa

Ocoroni

A Bacubirito

R. Fuerte

Charay

Mochicahui

SINALOA

A Culiacán

San Miguel

R. Sinaloa

Bamoa

Nio

Guasaua

R. Mocorito

Ahome

Tamazula

**Extent of the
1740
YAQUI
REBELLION**

México

Extensión maxima
de la insurrección

Battle Sites

Adapted from Luis Navarro García, *La sublevación yaqui de 1740* (Sevilla: 1966).

late May to the rebels' surrender in mid-October, except for the handful of yori prisoners they kept in the Yaqui missions, the rebels had cleared Ostimuri of all white people, vecinos and missionaries alike. Most of these fled to Alamos or safer towns further south. With all mining operations in the district at a standstill and all communications between Sonora and Sinaloa effectively cut off, the rebels enjoyed de facto control of the Yaqui–Mayo territory. At its height, the rebellion covered an area over 100 leagues in extension from north to south. Huidobro estimated the combined rebel strength at 12,000 to 14,000, organized into attack units of as large as 300 to 400. Jesuits contested these figures as somewhat exaggerated, pointing out that they were based on the assumption that all the Indians of the northwest had joined arms, which was not quite the case. Far from conducting a race war directed at annihilating the yoris, the rebels aimed their violence primarily at Spanish property. They sacked, burned, and pillaged the vecinos' homes, storehouses, mines, and chapels. They took slightly over 100 prisoners, mainly women and children, but killed surprisingly few men. Only in one case of a rebel assault were there as many as five Spanish casualties reported.[8]

The intense controversy surrounding the rebellion concerned the way Governor Huidobro handled the crisis at every accelerating step. To his detractors, he seemed capable only of reacting, but not of developing early on an overall strategy to suppress the rebels definitively. After the first attacks on Spanish property, he dispatched small contingents of ten to twenty presidial soldiers to pursue the raiders. When these retaliatory actions did little to dampen the rebel spirit, he tried *modos suaves,* or mild methods of pacification, that is, some form of reconciliation. Given his critical shortage of men and provisions, Huidobro explained later at his own defense, a full-scale military campaign was simply out of the question. Beginning in late April, he began visiting the rebel territory, starting with the relatively calm Fuerte pueblos and moving rapidly up to the more turbulent Mayo. But when he detected disturbing signs in the first Mayo pueblos, he interrupted the rest of his tour, noting that the villages were almost deserted as most of their residents had fled to the hills to join the rebels. Moreover, dissidents in these communities had stripped loyal gobernadores of their staffs of office, a clear sign of defiance. So instead of proceeding onward to the Yaqui, the governor turned back south to Camoa, undertaking the first of a series of much disputed retreats.[9]

Leaving sixteen men to garrison Camoa, Huidobro moved on to Baroyeca, which was some twenty-six leagues from the heart of the Yaqui territory, arriving on about May 14. While waiting for reinforcements from Sinaloa, he met with loyal Yaqui Captain General Gurrola, other loyal Yaquis, and several coyotes. Just when they were about to persuade Huidobro that it was safe to tour the Yaqui pueblos, he received the alarming report that at Santa Cruz in the Mayo some 3,000 armed rebels, including 50 Yaquis, had ambushed, disarmed, and humiliated a squadron of 70 Spanish auxiliaries.[10] Immediately afterwards another report arrived of yet another Spanish defeat at Echojoa, also in the Mayo. These setbacks convinced Huidobro that it was dangerous to tarry long at Baroyeca, let alone proceed on to the Yaqui.

While the governor was obviously losing his nerve, a few vecinos seized the initiative to negotiate an early peace. *Bachiller* or *licenciado* (degreed) Pedro de Mendívil, a priest and member of a prominent local Spanish family, Francisco Aldámez and Manuel de Valenzuela, all of Ostimuri, requested and received grudging permission from Huidobro to continue as planned to the Yaqui.[11] Arriving at Tórin pueblo on May 28, they found the people armed and ready for action, galvanized by the sudden news that Spaniards had killed Muni and Bernabé on their way home to Sinaloa. One Yaqui, Juan Calixto Ayamea, proclaimed himself leader of the movement to avenge the reported murders of their revered compadres. Until just recently, this Calixto had been commander of the loyal Yaqui auxiliary forces at Baroyeca, although he had also accompanied Muni and Bernabé to see Lieutenant Governor Peralta in 1738. According to Calixto and others, the two Yaqui leaders had left word before their departure that if they did not return within a specified period of time they could be presumed dead and their people were to avenge their murders. Although Mendívil tried his best to dispel what he was sure to be false rumors, and other Yaquis close to Muni, such as Luis Aquibuamea, denied that the two men had ever left such instructions, Father Nápoli chose to repeat the story, thereby lending much credibility to the rumor. In one instance, he even suggested that it was none other than Governor Huidobro who had ordered the treacherous murder of the returning travelers.[12] Under such a hostile atmosphere, Mendívil and company found it impossible to advance or even discuss their peace plans. For the duration of the rebellion, they remained in the Yaqui as prisoners, generally well treated.*

Mendívil's dismal failure only strengthened Huidobro's resolve to abandon Baroyeca as quickly as possible. At the time, he had with him

---

*It seemed ironic that, more than any of the many secular reports, the Jesuits sensationalized accounts of Yaqui brutality and prisoner treatment. According to them, for example, rebels raped a number of white women — wives of prominent vecinos — then dragged them off naked along with innocent children as captives in the Yaqui River. The motives for apparent exaggerations are unclear; after all, Jesuits had been the guardian of Yaqui morality for well over 100 years. Perhaps this was the Jesuits' way of illustrating what surely must have happened when missionary presence was abruptly removed from the Indian communities, in short, a not-so-subtle warning against secularization.

just seven soldiers and forty militiamen, most unarmed, sick, or maimed, according to his defense account. By May 31, Huidobro and most of the vecinos who had gathered at Baroyeca had retreated southward to Los Cedros, property of the prominent Lucenilla family. Then upon reports of the imminent arrival of Calixto with over 1,000 angry Yaquis bent on killing him, the governor fled south again to the important mining town of Los Alamos, arriving on June 2. There he fortified the city and barricaded himself behind its walls, not to emerge from his sanctuary until October. Keeping company with him were most of the fearful vecinos of Ostimuri. At Baroyeca, Los Cedros, and repeatedly at Los Alamos, Huidobro wrote the viceroy, the governor of Nueva Vizcaya, and the presidial captains of the north to send him reinforcements and provisions. He stated that he needed at least 500 men between soldiers and militia to suppress the massive, far-flung uprising. In the meantime, he maintained that he could do little but wait for help to come.

In the face of Huidobro's passivity and seclusion, others assumed the reins of leadership, particularly Sonora's *sargento mayor,* Captain Agustín de Vildósola. On July 6 and again on August 26, with less than 100 men each time, he repelled two massive, but uncoordinated, assaults on the town of Tecoripa lying on the Ostimuri–Sonora border. The first attack reportedly involved some 500 rebels, the second up to 2,000.[13] These defeats not only prevented the rebellion from spreading farther north to the restless Pimas Altos of Sonora, they gave rise to a desperately needed Spanish hero around whom the demoralized vecinos and Jesuits could rally. Together with additional crucial Spanish victories under local commanders in the Fuerte region south of Alamos, yoris began to gain the upperhand and turn the tide. Vecinos and especially Jesuits, who pointedly contrasted Vildósola to Huidobro as "a military man with character," credited the captain with the change in their fortunes. By late August, the first reinforcements arrived in Sinaloa, assuring success of a pacification which Vildósola had begun.

Further guarantee of peace came in the person of Bernabé, who arrived in Sinaloa on August 24, several weeks ahead of Muni. On September 7, Huidobro dispatched him to the Yaqui, where rebel chiefs had already extended peace feelers. On October 13, Bernabé and Pedro Mendívil accompanied a large group of prominent Yaquis to the governor's headquarters at Alamos, bringing in tow 103 Spanish prisoners. For days afterwards, new groups of repentant Yaquis came to surrender.

With additional reinforcements and newly activated militia units in Sinaloa and Sonora, Governor Huidobro was able to form ten companies of fifty men each. He assigned five for Alamos, four for Vildósola in

Sonora, and one for the Fuerte. When he finally moved out of Alamos in November, it was not to conduct an active military campaign but to consolidate the peace after the rebels' capitulation. Accompanied by Bernabé and the just arrived Muni, Huidobro left on November 3 for inspection tours of the Mayo and Yaqui missions. At the Mayo, he took the census in each pueblo, collected and burned confiscated weapons, which turned out to be mainly bows and arrows, and recovered and returned stolen Spanish property, including cattle. He also took many testimonies on the rebellion and its leaders. In one of his reports, Huidobro explained that he did not mete out severe punishments on the advice of a junta of his captains. They cautioned him against hasty and unduly harsh discipline of rebel leaders who had voluntarily surrendered. Before he departed the Mayo after a month's stay, he appointed a new captain-general as well as new gobernadores, stationing in addition a small peace-keeping force to supervise the safe return of missionaries.

Then Huidobro moved on to the most urgent business, that of securing the pacification of the Yaquis, undisputed leaders of the rebellion. After Muni and Bernabé had prepared the way for him, he spent the period from December 18 to January 3, 1741, inspecting the Yaqui pueblos, carrying out the same tasks he had accomplished in the Mayo. In taking the census, he noted that many Yaquis had traveled to the Sonora and Vizcaya mines for work, while others were navigating the supply boats to California or tending to their fields and ranches. In short, it appeared that many Yaquis had resumed routine peacetime activities.

While in the Yaqui, according to Viceroy Duque de la Conquista's instructions, Governor Huidobro promoted the loyal and cooperative Muni and Bernabé. He installed Muni as captain-general of the Yaqui mission and Bernabé as *alférez,* or militia captain, both with permission to use arms.[14] In addition, the governor granted the residents of Huírivis, Bernabé's native pueblo, and the most quiescent during the rebellion the privilege of carrying arms, further charging them with guarding the California boats and ferreting out escaped rebels.

Unfortunately for Governor Huidobro, he himself did not fare so well. On the last day of 1740, while still winding up his tour, none other than Captain Vildósola informed him that the viceroy had divested him of office and ordered him to proceed immediately to Mexico to answer serious charges of incompetence and cowardice. Huidobro knew then that he was the victim of an intense Jesuit political campaign. Leading the blistering offensive against him was the sharp-witted Father Provincial Mateo Ansaldo, rector of the Colegio de San Pedro y San Pablo in Mexico City. He and his colleagues pinned the blame for all of their troubles in the Yaqui mission during the past half decade on the governor. They found a receptive audience in Viceroy Duque de la Conquista, who happened to admire Father Ansaldo immensely. It also appeared that the new viceroy resented having to inherit the strange Yaqui visitors Muni and Bernabé from his deceased predecessor, the Archbishop-Viceroy Vizarrón. He agreed with the Jesuits that Huidobro had unwisely encouraged the Yaquis to accept Vizarrón's inopportune invitation. Hostility and resentment against Huidobro notwithstanding, most of all the viceroy wished to restore harmony and stability to the war-ravaged frontier province. In the mind, the contentious and irredeemably controversial Huidobro was simply not the best man for the job. Towards the end of peace, he removed Huidobro from the province, appointed Vildósola interim governor, and granted a general amnesty to the rebels.[15]

Huidobro's only defense was to return the Jesuits' assault volley for volley, blaming them in turn for the disintegration of order in his province. Actually, even before his dismissal from office, he had begun attacking the Jesuits. In several letters to the viceroy in September 1740, he listed a number of missionary policies and indiscretions which he believed had driven the Indians to rebel. These included the labor shortages going back to 1735; the Mena incident of 1736; Father Nápoli's despoilment of Yaqui churches; and the part Father Nápoli played in circulating the false, but inflammatory, rumors concerning Muni and Bernabé's murders.[16]

While the Jesuits and Huidobro battled out their differences in the high courts and through successive viceregal terms, Interim Governor Agustín de Vildósola continued the difficult task of securing the total submission of the Yaqui–Mayo peoples. Although he had condemned Huidobro on several occasions for softhandling rebel chiefs, shortly after assuming office he himself offered a conciliatory gesture by freeing some of the prisoners his predecessor had held in Tórin, Camoa, and Sinaloa. Then he reduced the large pacification force to 130 men, sending home the auxiliaries from Vizcaya and elsewhere. In March 1741, accompanied by veteran fathers Patricio Imaz, Miguel Fernández de Somera, and Bartholomé Fentanes as translators, Vildósola reinspected the Yaqui pueblos to pave the way for the permanent return of missionaries.[17]

The prerebellion generation of resident fathers, including González, Duque, Fentanes, and Nápoli, were too discredited to return to their posts. Instead, three new padres arrived at Ráum, Tórin, and Bácum: Fathers Agustín de Arriola, Francisco de Anaya, and Lorenzo García, who encountered no hostility at all from the Yaquis.[18]

Also during the March tour, Vildósola took a detailed census of the

Yaqui mission, noting down 15,700 persons "large and small"—not a small number considering the recent upheaval and the resumed migration to the mines.[19] He reported that a considerable number of Yaquis were still wandering in the marshes and open country, ignoring his entreaties to return to their pueblos.

After inspecting the mission, Vildósola visited the important Ostimuri reales and haciendas, such as Baroyeca, Río Chico, El Potrero, Río Grande, Los Cedros, El Sauz, and Carrizal, to encourage vecinos to return and resume mining and agricultural operations by promising them adequate armed protection. He posted garrisions of up to fifty men at various strategic locations: Buenavista, "entrance to the Yaqui" from upriver; Tecoripa, gateway to Sonora and the perennially restless Seris and Pimas Altos, who did not join the 1740 uprising; Camoa, close to the Mayos and the important town of Los Alamos; and El Fuerte, the southern border of the rebel-torn area.

In spite of these new and elaborate arrangements, Vildósola still felt uneasy, mainly because of Muni and Bernabé's strong presence in the pueblos. He was convinced that they were making plans for a new uprising, this time to include definitely the Seris and Pimas Altos, thus finally realizing the all-out race war that many Spaniards had feared. When in May and June 1741 both Father Arriola and the Buenavista garrison commander reported sighting Muni and Bernabé holding secret meetings in the sierra, the interim governor's worst suspicions appeared confirmed. He even suggested that these two Yaquis were Huidobro agents instructed to disrupt the delicate peace. Citing the alleged meetings as proof of sedition, Vildósola apprehended Muni and Bernabé in Tórin and had them swiftly executed and decapitated in Buenavista on June 23. Then he ordered their heads circulated in all the Yaqui pueblos as an ominous warning to their supporters and other dissidents. He followed up with the arrest of another forty-three suspected accomplices, including Juan Calixto Ayamea, self-proclaimed leader of the 1740 rebel forces. Fathers Arriola, García, and Anaya wholeheartedly supported Vildósola's decisive action in this matter, for they too harbored the same misgivings about Muni and Bernabé despite the total absence of real evidence against the two.[20]

The abrupt, brutal executions provoked sporadic acts of defiance, including the assassination of the new Yaqui captain-general, Hipólito Baheca, near Bácum. The prolonged instability prompted Vildósola in mid-1742 to conduct another tour of the Yaqui and Mayo missions, during which he exhorted the people to be loyal to the Crown and to work for the Spanish mines and haciendas.[21] Finally, two years after its outbreak, the 1740 rebellion could be said to have ended.

The complex question of responsibility for the rebellion initiated a protracted dispute between Jesuits and Huidobro.

The Jesuit case against Huidobro and cohorts was contained in two lengthy documents submitted to the viceroy as one package: Father Provincial Mateo Ansaldo's vituperative indictment against the governor and an anonymous report that assessed the "root, causes and progress" of the rebellion.[22] Written obviously for public consumption rather than internal use, these documents most emphatically exonerated the missionaries of all blame in provoking the 1740 crisis, contrary to what Huidobro and others had charged. Also, having contributed to Huidobro's recall in the first place, Ansaldo and colleagues strenuously opposed his petitions to return to his lifetime appointment as governor of Sonora–Sinaloa. They felt strongly that Huidobro, other local officials such as Alcalde Quiroz, and certain vecinos had actively encouraged the growth of a rebellious spirit among Yaquis that directly contributed to the audacious uprising of 1740. To them, the situation in the Yaqui mission notably deteriorated from the time of Lieutenant Govenor Mena's visit in 1736. The Jesuits pointedly characterized the demonstration against Mena as an "uprising," a clear mainfestation of growing insubordination. They also called attention to the fact that many of Muni and Bernabé's armed supporters were members of the Yaqui militia which Governor Huidobro had formed. The Pótam incident was like a dress rehearsal for the larger rebellion of 1740, the Jesuits argued, concluding that the whole unfortunate affair could have been prevented had Governor Huidobro disarmed and disbanded the Yaqui auxiliaries upon the first stirrings of trouble, referring to Muni's early complaints before Alcalde Quiroz in 1735.

In discussing the initial signs of rebellion, the Jesuits offered a somewhat curious account which begged for further explanation. According to them, in early 1740 an Apache Indian appeared in Ostimuri and began leading Yaquis to raid and plunder Spanish haciendas and ranches for cattle. There was no mention of how and why the Apache was in this area in the first place or what might have motivated Yaquis to join him in acts of violence uncharacteristic of their normal behavior. Neither did the Jesuits bring up the matter of floods, famine and desperately hungry Yaquis scouring the mountainside for edible foods, another uncommon Yaqui activity. It followed then that they made no reference to how Nápoli and the other fathers dealt with the crisis of hunger.

When the early raids generalized into widespread rebellion, Jesuits blamed Huidobro for having let the disorder get that far, much as they had censured him for not having punished Muni when he first reared his defiant head. In 1740, Jesuits maintained again that the governor could have prevented further deterioration of peace and order had he heeded early missionary warnings of trouble brewing in the Yaqui. He missed a second chance when he failed to deal a decisive first blow to the rebels. Then, even after he was forced to accept the fact of the uprising, he committed a number of other fatal errors. When Huidobro first toured the Mayo pueblos, he did not insist on rebels turning in their arms. At Baroyeca, Captain General Gurrola and other loyal Yaquis offered him their services but were unceremoniously rebuffed. Not only that, the Jesuits charged, but the governor stripped Gurrola of his office, replacing him with Muni partisan Luis Aquibuamea. In sum, according to the fathers, Huidobro was indecisive and unforgivably cowardly from the start, his pleas of insufficient men and provisions totally lacking in credibility. Most reprehensible were his hasty retreats, which left defenseless missionaries and vecinos to the rebels' mercy and which unnecessarily prolonged the crisis. An inordinate fear for his own life made him sacrifice the safety and welfare of others under his protection. The Jesuits also charged that, when some vecinos began demanding an investigation of Huidobro's irresponsible behavior, he threatened to kill anyone who dared inform on him. Even his estimate of rebel strength, a highly inflated 20,000, was but an attempt to justify his repeated claims of indefensibility. Father Imaz offered 15,000 as the absolute maximum, assuming all the Yaquis' neighbors had joined up in full force.

Another extremely sore point which Jesuits brought up was Huidobro's consistent failure to answer the fathers' desperate calls for armed escorts and protection, causing several of them unnecessary suffering. When Nápoli and others began issuing appeals for help in late 1739, Huidobro allegedly announced to them that he would not come to their aid "even if the [Yaqui] River becomes dyed with the padres' blood."[23] The story of the elderly Father Manuel Díaz was particularly poignant. Rebels captured him at his resident pueblo of Tesia in the Mayo, roughed him up, and dragged him off to see Chief Calixto. Although his rude captors eventually allowed him to leave for Alamos, the shock soon killed the poor father. Throughout his ordeal, Jesuits decried Huidobro's refusal to send military aid. Neither did he lift a finger to free Fathers Estrada and Mazariegos, imprisoned, respectively at the Mayo and Fuerte rivers. Father Fentanes of the Yaqui also had to fend for himself, finally escaping to the Mayo in time to join and support Father Díaz in flight to Alamos. These isolated incidents of harassment did not deter Jesuits from maintaining that the 1740 rebellion was aimed solely at Spanish rule and not at all against the mission system. They insisted that rebels "venerated and respected" the padres, while chiefs such as Calixto "spoke much against Spaniards." Huidobro's "bad government," Jesuits concluded, was the major cause of the uprising.[24]

The anonymous Jesuit report made other interesting observations and conclusions. For example, in the years preceding the crisis, Spanish greed for mission land probably had not reached the magnitude that Jesuits had dramatically projected On the other hand, Spanish pressure for more Indian labor was definitely acute and mounting. In highlighting the land question, the padres could well have been acting in anticipation of an inevitable conflict. They also perceived the close relationship between land and labor on the frontier: only by forcing sedentary Indians off the land and hence depriving them of their livelihood could Spaniards compel these Indians to work for them as "slaves" (the Jesuits' preferred term for wage laborer).

An oft-repeated and almost hysterical charge was to blame Huidobro for the presence and audacity of armed Yaquis in the mission. In fact, Indian militias or auxiliary forces recruited from the Jesuit and other missions were common throughout the northern frontier, where full-time professional soldiers were few and stationed far apart. For decades military governors and presidial captains had depended heavily on Indian auxiliaries to quell uprisings and maintain order. When Huidobro went to Baja California to help Jesuits suppress the Pericúe rebellion in 1735, he took with him a large Yaqui contingent. El Muni had so distinguished himself in military action against rebellious Seri and Tiburon Indians that the famous presidial commander, Juan Bautista de Anza, confirmed him as alférez of the Yaqui auxiliary. The fiscal or Crown attorney was among those who defended Huidobro on this charge, noting that the governor had hardly invented the practice of arming Indians for frontier defense and security.[25]

Through the years since 1740, Jesuit historians have uncritically accepted and faithfully paraphrased the Ansaldo and anonymous documents, thus continuing unabated the caustic personal attacks on Huidobro and alleged fellow conspirators. Writing at the end of the eighteenth century, the eminent Jesuit historian Father Francisco Javier described how "seditious elements" within the mission, "sponsored by several vecinos who needed them for their own private interests," instigated the uprising.[26] The early twentieth-century historian Father Gerardo Decorme was more elaborate in retelling the story.[27] He recounted how Governor Huidobro — "fatuous, lacking in talent, partisan and cowardly" — and "certain vecinos without conscience" maligned Jesuits in the most vicious manner and encouraged Yaquis to rebel.

Huidobro and friends intended to survey and distribute Yaqui land, replace missionaries with secular priests, and collect taxes and tithes, in short, to secularize the mission.

From the original documents and subsequent spinoff accounts, it becomes clear that underlying the uniform Jesuit interpretation of the 1740 uprising was the overriding fear and concern over secularization; all other problems and issues paled beside it in significance or were somehow related to this central conflict. The long buildup of tension and the revolt itself were more than just another Indian upheaval, but part of a larger threat with implications far beyond the event itself. The Jesuits did have grounds for apprehension when Huidobro became lifetime governor of Sonora–Sinaloa. Shortly after he took office, he suggested four far-reaching reforms for the mission system. Although ultimately not implemented, these proposals certainly represented attempts to undermine Jesuit power: (1) that each year residents of each mission pueblo nominate three candidates for the office of gobernador, from whom the resident father would select one; (2) that Indians be given their own plots or *milpas* according to the model of secular pueblos; (3) that communities or individual Indians owning more than twenty heads of cattle pay taxes of up to eight pesos a year; and (4) that some formal process be initiated to monitor the missionaries' conduct, for example, whether they taught the religious doctrines and treated the Indians kindly or whether, in fact, they abused their charges.[28]

To the missionary order, these were patently seditious ideas designed to erode Jesuit authority and to promote the cause of secularization. The Jesuit rector of Sinaloa opposed the first three measures as impractical and harmful to the Indians' interests. The ecclesiastical judge ruled the fourth inappropriate, insulting, and offensive to the *estado eclesiástico*. From this inausupicious beginning, Jesuits viewed practically every action Huidobro took and every decision he made as part of his grand scheme to depose them.

From the other point of view, Huidobro and other Crown officials had good reason to be wary of the Jesuits and to question the wisdom of their continuing hegemony in the region. Desirous of serving his King well—defending the "royal jurisdiction," in his own words—and thus advance his own fortunes as well, the governor has plans to develop the northwest's vast potential wealth by promoting secular economic interests. But he immediately ran against the powerful Jesuit edifice with all the accumulated weight of more than a century's head start. Lesser officials such as Alcalde Mayor Quiroz shared Huidobro's sentiments, especially since they formed part of the small, struggling secular Spanish population which had to compete fiercely with missionaries for the province's valuable resources, Indian land, and especially labor. In their reports, they frequently complained about the missionaries' arrogant and autonomous behavior: Jesuits defied the Crown's local representatives at will; encroached on secular jurisdiction whenever convenient; and, in general, disregarded any sovereignty other than their own.[29] Huidobro himself called attention to problems such as the tapisque issue and the Pótam incident as specific examples of the kind of highhanded Jesuit conduct he and his subordinates condemned. As a result of mutual apprehension and distrust, Huidobro and the Jesuits hardly experienced a moment of harmony during their years of awkward coexistence. As early as 1734, when the governor went to California to suppress the Pericúes, Jesuits there attacked him mercilessly for ineptitude, cowardice, and lack of cooperation, charges which presaged the even sharper condemnation of 1740 and afterwards.[30]

Later, in his own formal defense, Huidobro argued that he incurred Jesuit wrath because he took up the Indians' case of excessive workloads in the missions. He felt that the fathers could have prevented the demonstration against Mena had they paid some attention to the Yaquis' grievances. He also maintained that he never advised the Yaquis to disobey their missionaries when they first complained to local authorities in 1735. But—and this was the closest he came to openly advocating secularization—he did feel that the missions would prosper and progress if administered by clérigos or friars "not given to acquiring so much power, or to controlling everything."[31]

The irreconcilable differences between vecinos and missionaries underscored the problem of two fundamentally incompatible spheres of interest whose boundaries were drawing too close for further accommodation. It seemed that the governor anticipated by some thirty years several of the Crown's own motivations for expelling the missionary order from Spanish America. One primary official concern in the frontier region was to overhaul the relationship between church and state, between religious and secular interests. The deeply entrenched Jesuit hegemony in the northwest reinforced growing misgivings about a too powerful church. The fact that Huidobro's successor, Augstín de Vildósola, despite much effusive praise from the Jesuits in the beginning, soon found himself locking horns with his erstwhile friends was indicative of the situation.

In addition to Huidobro and most of his subordinates, Jesuits tended to assume that all vecinos also harbored prosecularization sentiments. The fathers looked upon any Spanish contact with Indians as attempts to poison innocent minds with anti-Jesuit ideas. After the 1740 uprising, they become more convinced than ever that exposure to Spanish ways and life style, primarily through the mines, would inevitably produce malcontented, rebellious Indians and upset the delicate order and stability that they had so carefully constructed over the decades. No doubt, most vecinos in the northwest engaged in mining and agriculture desired some relaxation of Jesuit control over the mission populations and their resources. Indians constituted their only source of labor and mission surpluses were practically their sole source of supplies. However, it was not at all clear that in the first half of the eighteenth century most vecinos had advanced from demanding a greater share of mission resources to actually clamoring for the ouster of Jesuits and the dismantling of the mission system. Moreover, it was doubtful that most vecinos would have promoted and then welcomed the devastating 1740 rebellion in order to achieve the limited ends they needed at that time. The Spanish population sustained the greatest damages in terms of both human casualties and especially property losses, which came to an estimated 20,000 pesos. There was no close accounting of the Spanish human casualties, but in no way could they have approached the grossly exaggerated figure of 1,000 to 3,000 that form one of the many myths surrounding the rebellion and that, in fact, some recent scholars have continued to accept uncritically.[32]

When Governor Huidobro lost his nerve early in the rebellion, several more stouthearted vecinos assumed the dangerous task of negotiating with the rebels, so eager were they to see the violence come to a quick end. Other vecinos constantly pressured him to act more decisively and responsibly to suppress the revolt. Although Mendívil's efforts failed to placate the rebels in April, he did have considerable influence over their decision to surrender in October. Just as Crown officials on the frontier were divided — best illustrated by the conflict between Huidobro and Mena — so Spaniards in general were far from constituting a united front, in sharp contrast to the Jesuits who did consistently speak with one voice, projecting unity and strength.

One other group to come under relentless Jesuit criticism was that composed of Muni, Bernabé, and their supporters, who set the fathers immediately on the defensive when they first stepped outside the mission with their complaints. Like most designers of closed communities, Jesuits preferred, indeed demanded, that the members settle their differences internally. To them, when on their own initiative these Indians discussed grievances with outsiders, even civil authorities officially charged with overseeing temporal affairs in the missions, they committed a gross act of insubordination and an unforgivable breach of confidence. In publicizing discord between missionaries and Indians, they only opened another door for unfriendly elements to interfere with mission affairs and challenge Jesuit hegemony. Naturally, the fathers felt deeply hurt and betrayed.

In Jesuit eyes, the greatest threats to their survival, even more than Huidobro, Quiroz, and their cohorts, were the Yaqui dissidents and their leaders, Muni and Bernabé. For to lose that crucial hold over the Indians themselves would have been tantamount to admitting failure in their missionary enterprise and to destroying the means for their continued existence on the frontier. Probably even before he and Bernabé sought out Alcalde Quiroz with their grievances, Muni had come under Jesuit suspicion for his frequent contacts with Spaniards in his capacity as Yaqui auxiliary captain. In time, Jesuits came to view the two leaders as critical collaborators in a nefarious conspiracy, more dangerous with their words than armed chieftains such as Calixto during the height of the actual revolt. For this reason it would seem, Fathers Nápoli and others gave much credence to and actively promoted the idea that Calixto turned rebel chief on the explicit instructions of Muni and Bernabé, the real leaders of the rebellion despite their absence from the province during its course. Jesuit actions before, during, and after the crisis bore a determination to destroy their credibility and continuing influence among their own people.

In Jesuit opinion, the two most significant events leading to the outbreak of 1740 both revolved around Muni and Bernabé. First, during Lieutenant Governor Mena's visit to the mission, they organized previously docile Yaquis to rise up and hence thwart the attempt to put a definitive end to the disturbances in the river area. Second, this time encouraged by Governor Huidobro, they accepted the viceroy's invitation to discuss their grievances with him personally in Mexico City. To the Jesuits' dismay and anger, both these events resulted in increasing the restless dissidents' insubordination and audacity. Finally, Jesuits were most certainly troubled and unhappy about the content of Muni and Bernabé's petition and the viceroy's reaction to it.

This petition is one of the few original Yaqui documents in existence. Presented to the viceroy in July 1739, it appeared to have been the work of Muni and Bernabé. Eventually, it was widely circulated not only within official circles in Mexico and Madrid, but among Jesuits as well, who made sure they obtained a copy.[33] Contrary to the Jesuits' worst fears, the statement was not a passionate plea for secularization. On the other hand, it was critical of certain missionary practices; its carefully, succinctly, and sometimes strongly worded list of grievances and reforms addressed problems that arose out of daily interactions with the fathers and their assistants in the pueblos.[34]

Muni and Bernabé began by asking the viceroy to clear their good names of the unjustly slanderous reputation which they had acquired and to absolve them of all charges leveled against them. They then urged the removal of Fathers Nápoli and González, who "by their bad counsel, terror and bad treatments" had caused all the trouble in the Yaqui mission. They followed this by a request to replace Captain-General Gurrola, and, "in accordance with the Law of the Indies," to expel from their pueblos Juan Frías, Ignacio Alipazaga, and all the other coyotes whom the fathers had brought in as assistants. Next Muni raised a personal grievance: he demanded the restitution of his land, which he claimed Father González had taken away as punishment for one of his alleged offenses. Another personal attack was directed at Lieutenant Governor Manuel de Mena: those Yaquis whom he had imprisoned in Pótam wanted compensation for the "damages" he had caused them. The petition did not specify the nature of these damages or the kind of compensation sought.

One of the requests in the petition would dispel any notion that Muni and Bernabé were anti-Jesuit in principle. They noted that, while "formerly" there used to be two padres for the four pueblos of Huírivis, Ráum, Pótam, and Belém, "now" there was only one. Hence they urged the immediate addition of another resident father as, they explained, one missionary could not administer adequately to the needs of so many families.

The remaining articles were undoubtedly those which caused the Jesuits the greatest degree of alarm and consternation. The grievances and proposed redresses were: that the Yaqui people not be deprived of the right to carry and use their traditional arms, which were bows and arrows;* that they not be forced to work in the mission without pay; that the padres not take away their land and convert it for other uses; that the freedom of their elections be guaranteed; that the Jesuit provincial protect them from excessive workloads in the pueblos, especially during the feast days and for transporting provisions to California; that they be allowed to sell their own produce to whomever they pleased; and that the padres not stop them from working in the mines. Finally, Muni and Bernabé requested the appointment of former Alcalde Quiroz as "Protector of Indians."

In asserting their right to bear arms, Muni and Bernabé could well have been reacting to persistent Jesuit attempts to strip them of this

---

*Apparantely, bows and arrows were about the only weapons that Yaquis used at this time, including the governor's auxiliary troops. During the demonstration against Mena and the 1740 rebellion, the Indians' "raised arms" consisted of bow and arrows.

privilege on the argument that weapons encouraged insubordination. The demands for free elections and the replacement of the unpopular, imposed Captain-General Gurrola referred to the longstanding, but illegal, Jesuit practice of interfering with local elections of native *justicias,* or officers. The request for payment for mission work echoed past challenges which Jesuits had successfully repelled — proposals which Spanish rivals for Indian labor had repeatedly raised. Equally disturbing to the Jesuits must have been the complaints about excessive workloads, for the wealth of their frontier missions derived from massive, unpaid Indian labor. Moreover, Muni and Bernabé's bold ideas regarding work were clearly seditious, for they questioned the unwritten principle of absolute Jesuit authority and infallible wisdom in managing Indian welfare.

Closely related to the question of work was an even more serious matter, that of the Yaquis' right to their own time, labor, and surplus. In demanding greater freedom to work in the mines and to sell some of their excess produce on their own, Muni and Bernabé struck at the core of the economic foundation of the Jesuit mission system, which was predicated upon total missionary control over the organization of labor and the allocation of resources and surpluses.

As a whole, however, although a number of the redresses sought were far-reaching, the petition fell short of arguing the case for actual and outright secularization of the missions. Without question, Muni and Bernabé represented Indian sentiments for greater independence from the Jesuits' paternalistic and autocratic rule. But while they asked for the removal of certain discredited and unpopular fathers, nowhere did they hint at the desirability of having secular priests. Nor did Muni and Bernabé demand the abolition of mission fields and ranches, even as they urged the reduction of workloads and payment for their labor, presumably so that they could enjoy more freedom to pursue other activities and some purchasing power. Contrary to rumors which Jesuits spread, nowhere in the petition did Muni and Bernabé propose that Indians pay tribute to the Crown, the single act most closely identified with secularization. In conclusion, it would appear that, while undeniably disgruntled with certain aspects of mission life and desirous of some fundamental changes, Muni and Bernabé remained basically appreciative of the benefits of living within the secure, well-organized, tax-free mission community under the watchful, but protective, eyes of the resident fathers.

Neither the petition nor any other piece of evidence could substantiate the Jesuits' serious and oft-repeated allegation that the "astute and ladino" Yaquis were mere pawns in evil Spanish hands. These insinuations denied any legitimate basis to the Yaquis' grievances and gave them little credit to act in their own interest, to be able to analyze and to react to their surroundings. The fact that Muni and Bernabé were out of the province during the actual uprising in 1740 or that they hastened home in August and September to aid in the pacification seemed almost irrelevant to their Jesuit detractors, convinced as they were that the two Yaquis' personal example and dangerous ideas were the principal sources of inspiration to the rebels. Jesuits might also have felt outraged by the one-sided focus of the petition: not a single grievance was filed against secular abuses. Yet given the nature of Yaqui contact with Spaniards and Spanish enterprises at the time, which was limited and extremely superficial compared to the longstanding, daily relationship with missionaries, the imbalanced emphasis is understandable. Friction between Indians and vecinos simply had not reached as acute a level as in the missions.

Within the highest official circles in Mexico, Muni and Bernabé found ardent defenders. One who became deeply involved with the controversies surrounding Huidobro and the Yaquis was the *auditor de guerra,* the Marquez de Altamira, a major counselor to the viceroy. His lengthy review of the 1740 rebellion implicitly challenged the Jesuit case against Muni and Bernabé. He argued that it was totally unreasonable to charge the two men with responsibility for causing the uprising. After all, they, along with certain vecinos, actively sought to pacify the rebels and apprehend the leaders. He also argued that the two Yaqui leaders could hardly be blamed for their trip to Mexico, since they went on the explicit invitation of Viceroy Vizarrón, whose successor in turn forgave them for their part in the Mena incident before sending them home to help with the pacification. In addition, the auditor noted, Muni and Bernabé partisans, such as Luis Aquibuamea, always remained loyal to the Crown and in many ways attempted to appease the rebels. Then he emphasized that the first disturbances in February 1740 did not even originate from Muni and Bernabé's pueblos of Ráum and Huírivis, but from Bácum, Cócorit, and several Mayo pueblos. Furthermore, even as the rebellion gathered adherents and spread far and wide, Ráum and especially Huírivis remained the most quiescent. Altamira also remarked rather sarcastically that it hardly made sense for Muni and Bernabé to travel the 400 arduous leagues to Mexico City to press for reforms only to leave behind instructions for an uprising. In their petition they did not ask for more than what they had always demanded from the local authorities in Sonora–Sinaloa. In the auditor's opinion— which the fiscal, the Crown attorney who also advised the viceroy, shared—these demands were not unreasonable or dangerous. Even if Interim Governor Vildósola did produce witnesses who testified that the Yaquis had planned to ask for the secular clergy to replace the Jesuits, this request in fact did not appear in the petition.[35]

The auditor made two other important observations. One, that three years after the rebellion, most of the reforms which Viceroy Duque de la Conquista had conceded to the Yaquis had not been implemented. Two, he disputed the commonly held notion that the rebellion was a race war aimed at exterminating the white man and Hispanic culture by noting that the rebels did not forget their Christian religion all during the turbulent months when they enjoyed de facto autonomy; they continued to attend mass, go to confession, and baptize their children. Altamira maintained that Fathers Estrada and Duque closed the mission churches and fled their Mayo and Yaqui pueblos in fear, despite Indian pleas to stay and administer to their spiritual needs. Rebels then begged in vain for Fathers Díaz and Somera to attend to them. It was only then that vecino and priest Mendívil reopened the mission churches for services, an act which, not surprisingly, was denounced by Jesuits.[36]

In 1744, after much deliberation over the voluminous and often contradictory evidence, Viceroy Fuenclara arrived at a decision regarding the fate of Governor Huidobro. First, he absolved Huidobro of all charges against him but then advised against reinstating him in office, appointing interim Vildósola as permanent governor instead. This decision actually reversed his own earlier opinion of 9 November 1743 to return Huidobro to Sonora–Sinaloa.[37] The change of mind reflected an obvious ambiguity on Fuenclara's part: while finding the evidence against Huidobro insufficient to indict him, he nevertheless recognized that the man had become too controversial to continue functioning effectively as governor of the remote northwest—a sensitive position that required trust from all quarters and constant balancing of competing interests. Implicit in this decision was also the opinion that, in the final analysis, no one party, Jesuit or Huidobro, was to be blamed solely for the disastrous crisis of 1740; much of the problem lay in precisely the "discord" between the two antagonists.

The 1740 rebellion had a different meaning to each of the various groups involved, giving rise to at least as many interpretations. The irreconcilable differences underscored the conflicts that provoked the crisis and that would remain unresolved for a long time afterwards. Yaquis, Jesuits, and Spanish vecinos all survived the upheaval, but it had also wrought or foreshadowed enough profound changes in relationships and circumstances to render impossible restoration of the status quo ante. For the missionaries most of all, the rebellion represented a significant turning point. Despite the return of resident fathers to the Yaqui and Mayo pueblos, Jesuits never regained their former preeminence in the northwest.

Myopically seeing the rebellion only through the filters of their own institutional interests, resisting the persuasion of other points of view, and interpreting practically every question raised about their practices and policies between 1735 and 1740 as one heinous Spanish plot to destroy them, Jesuits lacked the necessary flexibility to emerge from this conflict with their strength intact. In short, their intransigence contributed to their own eventual demise. They reached the unfortunate conclusion that the uprising was nothing more than Spanish manipulation of mindless Yaquis to sabotage the mission system and promote secularization, consequently failing to distinguish between different issues and aggrieved parties, to deal with mission tensions separately from Spanish pressures, and, finally, to offer concessions to both Indians and Spaniards that might have averted, or at least delayed, the violent reactions of 1740. To dismiss Muni and Bernabé's grievances as pure fabrications was to deny they had a firm basis within the mission, irrespective of Spanish pressures impinging on the system. In the end, Jesuit stubbornness left little room for Spaniards promoting their own economic development or for Indians desiring greater personal freedom to pursue their respective goals. Since the missionaries themselves seemed to have ruled out any possibility of compromise, they forced the hand of their secular adversaries, who saw no other solution than precisely that of secularization, that is, to eliminate Jesuit presence totally from the province.

The 1740 rebellion heralded the dawn of a new era, highlighted by the erosion of Jesuit hegemony in the northwest and the rising claims of secular political authority and economic interests. The Yaqui people could not escape being inextricably bound up with these changes, as the new power seekers made them an integral part of their designs. But as the Yaquis had already demonstrated, they were not about to be pliable tools to be used and manipulated without a clear and strong mind of their own.

The End of Jesuit Hegemony

After the suppression of the 1740 rebellion, not all the Spaniards who had fled Ostimuri returned promptly to repopulate their mines and haciendas. Save for a few hardy souls, the Real de Río Chico, once the prosperous cabecera of Ostimuri, was practically deserted; the Real de Baroyeca near the Mayo River fared somewhat better. Only four parish priests, including Pedro de Aragón of the Fuerte de Montesclaros, remained to serve the reduced number of vecinos. Many of Ostimuri's former residents had drifted to the new gold and silver mines recently discovered in Sonora, especially around San Juan Bautista and Aygame.[38]

Jesuits, however, did not abandon any of their missions in the province. Several more conscientious and sensitive fathers arrived to serve in the Yaqui and Mayo missions, the most eminent among them being

Father Juan Salgado. This was the last generation of missionaries in the area until the general expulsion in 1767. Father Salgado established residence in Huírivis, which was considered the most tractable of all Yaqui pueblos, attended to the nearby pueblo of Belém, which was being repopulated by dislocated Guaymeños and transplanted Pimas, and continued to supervise the remission of supplies to California.[39]

As for Governor Vildósola, despite a propitious initial rapport with the Jesuits, his tenure in office was even briefer than that of his ill-fated predecessor. His relationship with the missionaries began to sour barely two years after he took office, and his recall from office in 1747 was precipitated in large part by Father Vistador Juan Antonio Balthasar's repeated censures of his behavior and attitude.[40] Vildósola's successor, Diego de Parrilla, who took over in March 1749, had to deal with the first major rebellion of the Pimas Altos in 1751. Because he also disputed sharply with the missionaries over the correct handling of the crisis, which rivaled the Yaqui rebellion in magnitude and resembled its development in many ways, Parrila became another inevitable target of caustic Jesuit attacks.[41]

Not long after the Yaqui uprising and before the Pima Alto one, the deteriorating social and economic conditions of the northwest prompted the Crown to order a special inspection of the region. José Antonio Rodríguez Gallardo, appointed "Investigating Judge and Inspector of Presidios of Sonora and Ostimuri," arrived in Sinaloa in 1747. He traveled extensively throughout the province for over a year and filed several detailed reports. Gallardo's major proposals, to open up maritime trade between central Mexico and the northwest and to establish permanent Spanish towns, were intended to end the isolation of Sonora and Ostimuri from the core of New Spain as well as the insulation of the missions from the local secular economy and society. In many respects, the inspector argued for secularization without actually employing the term. He suggested, for example, that Spaniards and mixed bloods *(castas)* of "good moral character" reside in the mission pueblos, perhaps even serve as magistrates and overseers, and be granted land as enticement to settle. Only land could be the basis of permanence, Gallardo pointed out, whereas mines attracted Spaniards only as long as the exploitable ores lasted.

In general, Inspector Gallardo expressed a low opinion of the increasingly rebellious Indians inhabiting the frontier, but time and again he singled out Yaquis as exceptions despite their recent uprising. "The Yaquis are of a generous nature," he commented, "magnanimous and proud; they are very inclined towards religion, because even when they were in rebellion, they practiced many religious acts, as their wars were civil, or what was called during the time of Charles V, *'guerras de*

TABLE 2
Yaqui Census (1750s)

	1752*		1758**
Pueblo	Families	Individuals	(Families only)
Huírivis	942	3,800	1,168
Ráum	579	2,338	631
Pótam	555	2,503	604
Tórin	550	2,500	471
Vícam	800	3,500	900
Bácum	500	2,000	500
Cócorit	300	1,300	400
	4,226	17,941	4,674

*Report on Yaqui pueblos, Feb. 1752, in WBS/BLAC, Ms. no. 67, pp. 96–99.
**Ignacio Lizasoaín, Census of pueblos of Yaqui and Mayo, 1751–1757, taken in Santa Rosa de Bácum, April 14, 1758, in AGNM JHS 11–17.

comunidad.' " Moreover, he continued, they and their neighbors, the Mayos, were "more ladino than many Indians of Mexico... because, working in the mines, they learned the behavior and language of the Spaniards, and those who do not speak it, at least they understand it...." He noted further that their pueblos often appeared depopulated because so many of them were at the mines.[42]

Naval officer Fernando Sánchez Salvador made his inspection of the northwest immediately following Gallardo. He proposed outright the secularization, or what he termed the "mexicanization," of all the missions in Sinaloa up to and including the Yaqui. In support of his position, he noted that many of the missions were ready to pay tribute, although only the Indians of Culiacán were actually being assessed. In his detailed plan to reorganize the missions according to the "Mexican style and politics," referring to densely populated and intensely colonized central Mexico, he made no room for missionaries. Echoing Gallardo, he also took special note of the Yaquis, many of whom spoke Spanish "because of the large commerce and dealings they have with Spaniards." In Salvador's opinion, Yaquis should be encouraged to continue working in the mines for the "common good."[43] Both these inspectors made a strong case for far-reaching changes; however, for the time being the Crown silently shelved their reports, as if not quite ready to undertake large-scale reforms.

During troubled times, Jesuits also had the policy of conducting special investigations. Father Ignacio Lizasoaín inspected the Yaqui and Mayo missions several times between 1751 and 1757. Among his reports was a detailed pueblo-by-pueblo census for this period, counted by families.

Unfortunately, Lizasoaín did not specify how many individuals comprised these families. He did note, however, that the 1,168 households of Huírivis included 3,114 persons, for a ratio of approximately 1 to 2.7. In the absence of any other helpful information, a rough estimate for the total population in the Yaqui mission for this period, based on the Huírivis ratio, would place it around 12,600. Lizasoaín explained the low population with the observation that many Yaquis, especially of Bácum and Cócorit, the two uppermost pueblos and hence closest to Sonora, had absented themselves to the mines. Elsewhere in the same census report, he claimed that over 3,000 Yaquis had drifted to the reales. These comments confirmed the phenomenon that inspectors Gallardo and Salvador had already noted with some emphasis. The large-scale migration seemed to indicate that, despite strenuous Jesuit objections, Yaquis were asserting their independence and exercising their mobility with greater force and facility than ever before, thus confirming in turn that one consequence of the 1740 rebellion was, not surprisingly, the decline of Jesuit authority in the Yaqui mission.

Accelerating the erosion of Jesuit power was a new problem confronting the northwest. Shortly after 1740, Seri and Pima Bajo assaults increasingly threatened the security of this frontier. These rebellious Indians were occasionally joined by Pimas Altos, Suaquis, and others. Although Yaquis had traditionally volunteered for, or been pressed into, military services for the state, for the first time they assumed the defense of their own mission against marauding *bárbaros,* or barbarians. Gradually, during the next two decades, the area of defense expanded to include a wider region bounded by the Apache frontier to the north and the Fuerte River to the south. In one of Father Lizasoaín's reports, he claimed that over 100 Yaquis had been killed by various rebel attacks on the mission.[44] The presidio of Buenavista changed from its original and primary purpose of policing the Yaqui pueblos to combatting Pima and Seri rebels. But since the presidio had only fifty regular soldiers, Yaquis themselves made up the bulk of the defense and expeditionary forces. The mission also provided most of the food and other necessities for the military campaigns. These new demands obviously diverted many human and material resources from routine mission operations and needs.

This new state of military emergence gave prominence to a position within the Yaqui mission which appeared relatively new; only during the 1740 rebellion did the post of captain-general begin to receive attention. It is not clear when this office was first created in the Yaqui. Neither Father Pérez de Ribas nor his immediate successors in the seventeenth century ever mentioned the establishment of such a position. But if it was a relatively recent addition to the Yaqui mission, it had always been an integral part of the Sonoran missions, whose stance of frontier defense necessitated such a military officer from their inception. Yet missionaries never felt comfortable with the native captain-general, probably because the institution contradicted their policy of not elevating anyone within the mission to a position of overall authority and great prestige. In his denunciation Father Juan Nentuig reflected his colleagues' uneasiness:

> The office of captain general is not for the good of religion because the Indian, however good he may be, when he is praised or given any rank, from humble he becomes proud, from diligent he becomes negligent, for he thinks that there is nothing more to aspire to. He ceases to be docile and becomes capricious and obstinate, and the worst is that he becomes a bad Christian.[45]

Compounding the Jesuits' apprehensions over the rising status of the captain-general was a second source of anxiety, which was the growing presence and involvement of civil authorities in the affairs of the mission. This development also had its roots in the recent past, when local officials began recruiting Yaquis for expeditionary campaigns, and later, when they assumed primary responsibility for suppressing the 1740 rebellion. Their importance increased as the need to defend the mission arose. Even the missionaries recognized the urgency of cooperating closely with civil military authorities to protect the Yaqui pueblos. Father Salgado dutifully reported to Governor Juan Pineda or Captain Lorenzo Cancio of the Buenavista presidio on the mobilization of Yaqui auxiliaries and the preparation of provisions for the sorties against the rebels.[46] The relationship was always strained, however, because since the days of the hapless Governor Huidobro Jesuits scarcely disguised their deep contempt of all persons holding secular offices on the frontier: "The governor is almost invariably an unschooled officer sent out from Spain, who is sometimes also unfit for military duty." As for alcaldes and captains, "... captains are generally former employees of merchants and poor store clerks. The post of alcalde is often attained by the lowest type of person." So although the fathers acknowledged the need to defend the mission and in spite of the Guadalajara Audiencia's longstanding rule that civil officials should have complete jurisdiction over temporal affairs in the missions, Jesuits maintained whenever possible that these ill-qualified men should "have no authority over the Indians."[47]

A persisting cause of serious concern for the missionaries was the continued migration of Yaquis to the mines. Even the Seri, Pima and Apache raids did not deter Yaquis from leaving, so long as a sufficient number of them remained behind to defend the pueblos. In 1759, the discovery of gold near Soyopa, on the middle course of the Yaqui River in Sonora, raised the demand for mine workers; the placer method for gold required a large labor force. The Real de San Antonio de la Huerta was soon crowded with some 5,000 persons, most of them Indian laborers. Even women and children were employable in the tedious task of washing for gold.[48] In addition to Soyopa, gold placers were discovered along other arroyos of Sonora in a stretch of 140 leagues from the Yaqui to the Cuquiarachi River. Bishop Tamarón y Romeral, who undertook a series of visits to the western half of his spiritual domain from 1759 to 1761, confirmed the predominance of Yaqui mine workers in Sonora. In San Antonio de la Huerta alone, the local priests reported to him that there were 250 permanent Spanish families and 2,561 floaters, of whom about 2,000 were Yaquis.[49]

The bishop produced a detailed census of the Yaqui mission for the period from 1759 to 1761, summarized below:

TABLE 3
Yaqui Census, 1759–1761

Pueblo	No. of Families		No. of Individuals	
Cócorit	400	(400)[a]	1,900	
Bácum	490	(500)	2,530	
Tórin	840	(471)	2,645	
Vícam	1,002	(900)	3,618	
Pótam	804	(604)	2,458	
Ráum	843	(631)	2,684	
Huírivis	1,336	(1,168)	—	(3,114)[b]
	5,715	(4,674)	15,835+	

[a]Father Lizasoaín's figures (1751–1757).

[b]For some unexplained reason, Huírivis was the only pueblo for which Tamarón gave no total population figure; yet it was the only one for which Lizasoaín did give a total. According to Tamarón's report, the number of families in Huírivis increased; so if we accept at least Lazasoaín's figure of more than 3,000 for Huírivis, then the total population in the Yaqui from 1759 to 1761 would be around 19,000.

SOURCE: Pedro Tamarón y Romeral, *Demostración del vastísimo obispado de la Nueva Vizcaya,* 1765, ed. by Vito Alessio Robles (Mexico: Antigua Lib. Rob. de Porrúa, 1937), pp. 244–46.

Even though a population of 15,000 to 19,000 (see footnote to Table 3) was quite respectable, the bishop cautioned that it fell far short of representing the actual number of Yaquis alive. For every Yaqui found in the mission there were two more:

who are wandering outside, dispersed in these provinces, and in Nueva Vizcaya, [it was found] that if we add those who are away from their homeland, it would comprise several thousand. In Soyopa alone there are no less than two thousand, ... in Saracache, which was discovered later, there is another multitude ... in Chihuahua, there is a large number, having already formed a pueblo.... [50]

Moreover, the mission population was not all Yaqui, but included Indians of other nations. Some could have been Mayos, whose number in their own pueblos totaled an otherwise inexplicably low 3,883 individuals.[51] Other Indians were newly pacified rebels, notably Pimas and some Seris, whom missionaries had been relocating in Yaqui pueblos for some time, especially in Huírivis and Belém. The bishop also made a significant reference to a number of Spaniards found in the Yaqui mission. Unfortunately, he did not clarify whether these were transients, traders, soldiers directing the defense, or actual colonists putting down roots.

Jesuits seized at the opportunities offered by the bishop's visits to complain about the excessive migration of Yaquis and other Indians to the mines, but ultimately to no avail. They tried to discredit conditions in the camps, depicting the wages as low and the work abysmal. They also revived one of their favorite arguments:

Those [Indians] who have once tasted a life of license in such places [reales] seldom come back to their villages, and, if they ever come back, they are the Devil's own leaven, for they show the others the vices they have learned and stimulate them to go and do likewise. ... It is useless for the missionary fathers to send for them; for they are shielded by their employers and by those whose duty it should be to oblige them to return.[52]

This last reference was an obvious reference to uncooperative civil authorities.

After his own judicious study of the situation, Bishop Tamarón y Romeral found he could not concur with the Jesuits' opinion:

I deem it convenient to permit the Yaquis to continue their inclination. They are very ambulatory, leaning towards the mines. They are most useful in all aspects of gold and silver mining, in which they are of great advantage. They are very strong in these tasks. They know the veins in the mines and discover them. For these reasons, all the miners seek them out, because they are hard working and able-bodied, and they are appreciated everywhere and the result is for the common good.

The emphasis clearly was on the common good, which should take precedence over Jesuit imperatives, the bishop seemed to imply. The general welfare could be served in another way by permitting Yaquis their mobility, Tamarón continued, because serious curtailment of their freedom might provoke another devastating uprising.* Moreover, given their past ability to mobilize a large fighting force in short time, it was not desirable to encourage this "proud, strong and warlike" people to congregate in their mission, "because all together they would be capable of annihilating these provinces, and much more if allied with Seris and Pimas." This same concern, the bishop explained, was what prompted him to "see to it that [Yaquis] are well treated in Vizcaya and that they form their own pueblos [in the mining camps] . . . and whose welfare I have entrusted to the secular priests."[53] If the Jesuits were able to muster a response to his elaborate justification for supporting continued Yaqui migration to the mines, the bishop did not record it. It seemed that the fathers retreated into a new mood of resignation, unable to redirect the course of events that had drifted out of their control.

Bishop Tamarón y Romeral's lengthy report constituted part of the voluminous documentation the Bourbon monarchy compiled on the north and northwest in preparation for a major overhaul of its colonial system and economy. As conceived by master reformer José de Gálvez, the plan for New Spain's unstable, but potentially lucrative, mining frontier was to expand its economy and stimulate Spanish colonization, which should then produce greater revenues for the Crown. In 1766, Gálvez arrived for a thorough inspection of the viceroyalty.[54] Troubled that richly endowed provinces such as Ostimuri had so few Spanish residents and was economically so stagnant, the visitor general consulted with local authorities as to the best course to remedy the lamentable situation. Captain Cancio of Buenavista presidio was among those who submitted a proposal for the invigoration of Ostimuri. His reforms, not surprisingly, focused on the missions, the dominant and most stable institution in the region.

Cancio's suggestions were reminiscent of those advanced by inspectors José Antonio Rodríguez Gallardo and Fernando Sánchez Salvador some twenty years earlier. The missionaries would have been horrified if they had heard Cancio, their close partner in the defense of the Yaqui mission, propose to Gálvez that:

> . . . a competent number of Spaniards be aggregated to the Indian pueblos established on the margins of the Yaqui; to them we reward something in the beginning, and grant them land and water,

---

*Ironically, Jesuits often argued the opposite: that secularization would disrupt peace and order on the frontier and most certainly precipitate Indian uprisings; *see* page 84 above. However, the Jesuits' expulsion in 1767 did not result in massive Indian rebellions, as the present discussion reveals.

so that they can subsist and develop the cultivation of the fields; so that in this way, the reales de minas would have the necessary provisions and buy from them....In a few years, the Spaniards would marry with the Indians, who would forget their barbarous customs and abominable vices.[55]

Without using the term *secularization* outright, but by promoting Spanish self-sufficiency in agricultural needs and by advocating formal miscegenation between the races, Cancio's proposals would ultimately destroy the mission system.

Indeed, Visitor General Gálvez's first significant reform was directed at the Jesuits, and, when the Crown decreed in 1767 the expulsion of the entire Jesuit order from its American colonies, the missionaries' entrenchment in the northwest was definitely an important contributory factor. The kind of hegemony Jesuits had exercised in this region no doubt heightened the strong sentiment in Spain and in America that the fathers' enormous political and economic control considerably held back the full development of secular interests and society.

Interestingly, despite the Jesuits' dominant position, their expulsion from the northwest proceeded in a relatively quiet, orderly manner, marred by only a few incidents. In July 1767, Viceroy Marqués de Croix transmitted the expulsion decree to Governor Pineda, who in turn instructed his subordinates to inform the missions. The Ostimuri and Sinaloa officials assured their Indians of Crown protection and of the arrival of secular priests to replace their departed missionaries. They would also be free to leave their pueblos and live with Spaniards if so desired. Their gobernadores were to take interim charge of temporal and spiritual matters, maintain law and order, guard the community granaries, measure out rations for field hands, make sure that seeds for the next planting were distributed, supervise the harvests, in short, ensure the continuation of regular activities in the missions.[56]

Captain Cancio took charge of evacuating the ten missionaries in the Yaqui and Mayo to Mexico City via Guaymas port.[57] Despite some initial anxiety over possible adverse reaction to the sudden expulsion, Cancio met with actual little resistance from either Jesuits or Indians.[58] He was able to persuade the priest and vicar of Alamos, the enduring Pedro de Aragón, to proceed immediately to the Yaqui and take temporary charge of spiritual matters.[59] To each Indian pueblo, Cancio assigned a special commissary who, with the assistance of the native gobernador, was to take an inventory of the goods and cattle. This property would then revert to the control of the Crown under the title of "Temporalities of the King."[60] The measure was designed to protect the Indians, after abruptly losing their Jesuit protectors, against loss of their properties to greedy and unscrupulous Spaniards.

On September 19, when the Jesuits embarked for Guaymas from the port of Las Cruces near Huírivis, Cancio heard rumblings of disturbances in the Yaqui. After a quick tour of the lower four pueblos, he dispelled fears of an imminent uprising, reporting that he found the people "with a great tranquility, very happy with the removal of the fathers...."[61] The captain's anxiety heightened somewhat when in December new rumors circulated about Jesuits who were still waiting in Guaymas fomenting dissidence among Yaquis who had contact with them. Consequently, Cancio immediately issued orders to the commander of the Guaymas garrison to "in no way permit [Jesuits] to speak with Yaquis or any other person from the outside."[62] The captain later explained why he had been so concerned about the Yaquis. In May, just before the missionaries were rounded up, spring floods had destroyed most of the mission crop, threatening famine; fortunately, the people survived on the foods stored up from previous harvests.[63] The evacuation from the Yaqui was finally completed without further complications.

In view of the developments since 1740, the Yaquis' calm acceptance of the Jesuit expulsion after two-and-a half centuries of tutelage was not entirely surprising. First of all, Yaquis had become morally and materially less dependent on the mission, whose life or economy was no longer the only viable choice open to them. The Spanish mines offered to more and more Yaquis an alternative means of livelihood and a different social frame of reference. Second, for those remaining in the pueblos, defense of their homes against Seri and Pima assaults became the primary preoccupation. In this military task, presidial captain Lorenzo Cancio and the Yaqui captain-general, rather than the resident fathers, provided the leadership. For the first time in mission history, Jesuits played only a supporting role in a key mission function, preempted from the position of highest authority. By 1767, no longer a crucial or predominant force in the lives of Yaquis, the Jesuits' sudden removal did not cause a serious disruption, at least for these Indians.

The quick and smooth transition from missionaries to secular priests also softened the impact of the expulsion for Yaquis. Vicar Aragón's temporary guardianship soon gave way to the permanent installment of the priest Joaquín Valdés and his four assistants. By cooperating closely with the ongoing campaign against marauders, resettling pacified Pimas in Belém pueblo, and taking charge of mission production and properties, these priests assured the continuity of all vital functions in the Yaqui.[64]

Finally, the character and integrity of Captain Cancio himself facilitated the peaceful transition to the end of Jesuit rule. In his long and active association with the Yaqui people, Cancio had earned their respect and loyalty. Again and again, he would demonstrate to them his genuine interest in their welfare. For example, when vecinos began exerting pressure on Yaqui resources, Cancio reminded them sternly that commissaries were placed in the missions precisely to protect the Indians and their properties from despoilment until Visitor General Gálvez should decide how best to dispose of them. He warned them that no one was to disrupt the "beautiful plan of equity and justice" which the King had promised the Indians in return for their allegiance.[65] On another occasion, in March 1769, Cancio became incensed when informed that *Sub-delegado* Eusebio Ventura Beleña had authorized the Yaqui commissaries to sell some of the mission goods. He promptly issued a strong protest to Beleña and begged him to rescind his order:

> On the news of selling the cattle and horses of the mission, it would make such a terrible impression on the spirits of the Indians that would immediately lead us to a terrible and lamentable consequence. I have express orders from the Most Excellent Señor Viceroy and the Most Illustrious Señor Visitor General not to permit the sale of any kind of cattle and horses.[66]

Captain Cancio did not even hesitate to dispute the wisdom of decisions unfavorable to Yaquis when they came from the highest authorities. When Gálvez instructed him to organize tapisques of Yaquis and Mayos for Baja California mines, he balked at the plan, citing the Yaquis' grave reservations about going to such far and inaccessible places. Traveling to Nueva Vizcaya mines was acceptable because they could easily find their way home from there, Cancio explained patiently. For it was important to Yaquis that they be able to return home rapidly for major festivals, which they continued to celebrate after the Jesuit expulsion with "even greater gusto and numbers." Why not recruit vagrants and Spaniards with no legitimate occupations instead, the captain suggested. Finally, he pleaded with Gálvez that, if Yaquis had to be sent, then rotate the work teams every four months and ensure their good treatment in California.[67]

Besides his own genuine concern for the Yaquis' well-being, Captain Cancio needed their loyalty for the ongoing campaign against rebellious Indians. Time and again, the captain praised the efficiency of his Yaqui deputy, Calixto, and his 100 auxiliaries in rounding up rebels in the vicinity of the mission. He also posted Yaquis alongside presidial soldiers throughout Ostimuri province. In May 1769, Gálvez himself arrived in Sonora to launch an all-out campaign which, hopefully, would bring about the definitive pacification of the interior of the northwest, leaving only the Apache frontier yet to be dealt with.[68] He began the campaign by offering a general amnesty to those rebels who surrendered within forty days. But despite several extensions of the deadline, in the end only about 100 families had consented to be resettled in Belém under the sponsorship of Father Valdés.[69] In June, the visitor general also had to contend with the unexpected uprising of Indian pueblos on the Fuerte River; they apparently protested efforts to ship them off to the California mines.[70] Ironically, Cancio had predicted just such a consequence had Yaquis been drafted against their will. What made the Fuerte revolt even more alarming were rumors that Yaqui and Mayo agitators had been seen in the area, promising the rebels that their people were ready to join up. Fortunately for Gálvez and the Spaniards, the alliance did not materialize, and the disturbance was contained within the Fuerte River. During this crisis, Cancio expressed immense confidence in the Yaquis, repeatedly assuring Gálvez that he had nothing to fear from these loyal Indian subjects. When Cancio organized the expeditionary forces against the Fuerte rebels, he actually included over 800 Yaquis.[71] Finally, two years, many thousand pesos, and an apparent mental breakdown later, Gálvez felt sufficiently confident to call off the campaign — a combination of appeasement and military force — even though not all rebellious Indians had been subjugated.[72] Nevertheless, he needed to move on to other important reforms.

Even while Gálvez was conducting the last of the campaigns, he drew up plans for the political and social reorganization of those Jesuit missions which had not been transferred to Franciscan hands. These included the Yaqui and all missions south of it. Gálvez's reforms were designed to redefine the relationship between Indians and vecinos, in effect, to integrate the indigenous peoples socially, politically, and economically into colonial society at large. On 23 June 1769, he issued the first decree outlining changes on two fronts: one, the division and assignment of mission lands to Indians and Spaniards; two, the incorporation of Indians into the tribute system.[73] Local authorities received explicit instructions to set aside land for the Indian township, commons and pastureland, the parish priests, and the households, with the captain-general, the gobernadores, and the captains and soldiers of the militia company entitled to larger plots. Granted in perpetuity by the Crown, the Indian land grants could not be alienated, mortgaged, or damaged in any way. Land left over from the initial division would be set aside for future heads of households. Land outside the area designated for Indians would be divided into lots and sold to legitimate Spanish colonists who had already established themselves in the vicinity or Spaniards of good moral character with sincere intentions to settle down. It was the King's hope, Gálvez explained, that Indians and Spaniards would learn to live together as brothers, socially and commercially, in mutual aid and for the common good.

A special commission drew up a list of Indian and other tributaries. Indians had to pay fifteen *reales* per year, whereas vagrants and mulattoes were subject to twenty reales. The captain-general and gobernadores of each mission were responsible for the collection of tribute payments, due each year at the end of June and December. As reward for services rendered, they received four percent of the tribute collected. Moreover, as further recompense for performing their duties, the captain-general, officers, and soldiers of the militia company were exempted from tribute for life and the gobernadores for the duration of their tenure in office.

As to how the Yaquis greeted these far-reaching reforms, there were certain indications that a combination of natural disasters and Yaqui obstinance thwarted their implementation. In January 1771, Gálvez found it necessary to reiterate the original decree as well as issue new instructions on how exactly to divide the land into private parcels and assign them. Many years later, in August 1778, Intendant Governor Pedro de Corbalán* had to reissue this second, revised set of instructions.[74] Part of the difficulty in dividing the land in the Yaqui, the 1771 document pointed out, was the constant shift of available arable land on the margins of the river, a problem caused by the yearly floods. What was rich, cultivable land one year might become completely inundated and, unavailable or unusable the next. The same document also expressed frustration with attempts to collect tribute. Intendant Corbalán reported with exasperation that, in December 1771, he had not received even one-fourth of the payments due in June, attributing the difficulty again to the floods which had left most of the pueblos in desperate straits. The viceroy cautioned him to proceed delicately so as not to arouse the Indians unduly.[75] These technical problems certainly complicated implementation but could not have been the only obstacle to the reform program. Yaquis themselves appear to have responded minimally, if at all, to the reforms, making it necessary for high authorities to reissue and revise the original decree twice during the course of ten years. Significantly, at the end of the colonial period half a century after Gálvez's first proclamation, Yaquis had not become private cultivators coexisting happily with Spaniards and obediently paying tribute.

One way Yaquis silently thwarted the reforms was to move with ever greater alacrity to the mines of Sonora, creating with their constant

---

*The Intendant Governor was the chief administrative official of the reorganized political unit for the northwest, the Intendancy of Arizpe.

mobility a demographic instability that hindered reform efforts. In 1771, Cieneguilla, one of the northwest's most lucrative mines, was discovered. By 1772, the camp had over 7,000 persons, half of whom were Indian laborers. Yaquis, Mayos, and other Indians fled there to escape the new tax burdens and seek a new livelihood.[76] As in the past, Yaquis were singled out for praise as the "most industrious and civilized people," always dependable for providing workers for the mines.[77] For the duration of the colonial period, this movement of Yaquis to the mines continued unabated. In 1786, Viceroy Bernardo de Gálvez in his lengthy instructions for governing the Internal Provinces — the Bourbon's new title for the revitalized northwest — directed Commander General Jacobo Ugarte y Loyola to protect the roads with troops so that Yaquis could pass safely to the new Sonoran mines of Cieneguilla, Bacoache, and Zaracache. In this way, the viceroy explained, "we will benefit more abundantly by the riches of the minerals now lost through the scarcity of laborers and abandoned because of Indian hostility," referring to the relentless Apache raids.[78] The viceroy's policy of facilitating Yaqui travel implicitly sanctioned their participation in the mining economy as the top priority, superseding any obligation to remain in their pueblos and conform peacefully to the political reforms which his uncle, the Visitor General and later Minister of the Indies José de Gálvez, had formulated. Indeed, the viceroy did not once bring up the problematic Gálvez program, perhaps realizing that the two goals could not be successfuly pursued at the same time. Given that the highest importance was accorded the mines in the Bourbon economy, it was clear which policy had to take precedence.

Available population figures illustrated clearly the demographic fluctuations in the Yaqui. In 1784, resident priest Valdés reported a high of 7,900 families, or 23,070 individuals.[79] He cautioned at this time that any census figure could only be tentative, given the Yaquis' propensity to move. After Viceroy Gálvez's 1786 directive, the numbers residing in the pueblos had declined sharply to 16,000 by 1791. Another observer in the first years of the nineteenth century noted a rise, to 20,000.[80]

This heavy and indispensable contribution to the colonial work force did not mean, however, that Yaquis abandoned their community and culture. In essence, what they did was to continue the rotational pattern of movement between missions and mines. At any one time, a significant number of Yaquis stayed in the pueblos to sustain a vigorous society and viable subsistence economy. Those away always made sure to return periodically to renew social and cultural ties. Homeward-bound Yaquis were especially evident just before the important feast days, which, in Bishop Antonio de los Reyes's words, they zealously celebrated "to the extreme of superstition."[81] So with the support of Valdés and his assistants, Yaquis managed to retain a modified version of the old mission community. Their pueblos constituted the major exception to the general pattern of rapid disintegration in the old northwest missions. In Sonora especially, Spanish vecinos had entered former missions to cheat the defenseless Indians in trade and to demoralize them with alcohol.[82]

The original eight Yaqui pueblos remained intact, each with its traditional gobernador. Proposed for office by the resident priest and formally nominated by the alcalde mayor of Ostimuri, his immediate superior, the gobernador's expanded responsibilities included overseeing the community plot and ranch and guarding the *bienes de comunidad,* or communal goods.[83] Each gobernador received ten to twelve assistants, instead of the one or two in the old days, to aid him in his duties and to instruct the young in the doctrines. More assistants were needed than in Jesuits' days because, as the priests explained, Yaquis had dispersed themselves over a wider area, having partially reverted to their aboriginal custom of living near their cultivated fields.[84]

The Yaqui captain-general position also survived with enhanced power and prestige. Upon conclusion of the antirebel campaign in 1769, José de Gálvez institutionalized the Yaqui militia company and appointed the captain-general commander of this "Company of Nobles."[85] Successive holders of the office gradually defined its authority in the post-Jesuit political order. An exemplary figure was Captain-General Felipe de Jesús Álvarez, who served during the last ten years of the eighteenth century. He developed a keen sense of the boundaries of his jurisdiction and fought strenuously to preserve Yaqui autonomy within their own territory. In a letter he wrote to Lieutenant-Captain José María Areñas of Ostimuri, he bluntly reminded his nominal superior that, since he, Areñas, had authority only over Spaniards outside the mission, he should stop interfering with matters which concerned Yaquis inside the mission. The dispute apparently lingered on, for ten years later, Areñas's superior complained to even higher authorities that the Yaqui captain-general was pushing for "more jurisdiction than he ought to exercise."[86]

Álvarez's assertion of Yaqui autonomy was facilitated by the fact that very few Spaniards had moved permanently into Yaqui territory, another indication that the Gálvez reforms had not succeeded. This enabled Álvarez to insist on a sharp distinction between his domain and that of the nearest civil authority. The Yaqui pueblos, which in themselves constituted one of five political districts in Ostimuri, was described as "without another Spanish settlement or rancho." Actually, several Spanish and mestizo individuals could be found in or near the pueblos, but the priests regarded them as "vagrants and bums." Most of them engaged in trade with the Yaquis, passing in and out of the area on a transitory basis.[87]

Under Father Valdés's relaxed supervision, Yaquis in the pueblos led a peaceful life for the duration of the colonial period, never once rebelling or raising problems other than the occasional jurisdictional dispute that called for the attention of local authorities. Innovations which the priests introduced included a primary school in Pótam, where, in marked departure from Jesuit practices, they taught in Spanish. Unlike their missionary predecessors, these priests spoke little or no Yaqui.

Valdés was justifiably proud of achievements in the artisanal area. Not only did he build a "factory of looms and spinning wheels for woolen and cotton," but also brought in a master craftsman from Guadalajara to improve the Yaquis' skills. Later on, to increase both the quantity and quality of raw materials for the new weaving industry, he taught Yaquis how to cultivate the *lino,* or flax seed. So skilled did Yaquis become in this endeavor that they were able to clothe themselves adequately and had a little surplus to sell to Spaniards.[88]

The priest also boasted of extraordinary successes in his management of the community ranches. At the end of the century, he proudly claimed a total of 24,435 head of cattle, sheep, horses, and beasts of burden in Huírivis, Ráum, Tórin, and Bácum.[89] Yaquis themselves cultivated the traditional crops of maize, beans, and wheat, raising usually two harvests a year, and planted new ones, such as sugar cane and several varieties of fruit trees. Produce from the community plots went mainly towards maintenance of the churches and resident priests, who had received practically no financial assistance from the Crown, despite the promise of yearly synodals.[90]

Not surprisingly, the Yaquis' level of agricultural production was not nearly as high as during the Jesuit heyday. After providing for their internal needs, there remained only a small surplus for trade with outsiders. Rather than an ill reflection on their diligence and abilities, the lower productivity could be explained by changes in circumstances and purposes. First, the heavy migrations considerably reduced consumption needs in the pueblos. Second, Jesuits took with them the rationale for large-scale surplus production, for with their departure in 1767, Yaquis were no longer committed to supplying regular and prodigious quantities of provisions to new Jesuit missions.

This dual existence of working in the Spanish mines and, at the same time, of sustaining a separate autonomous society in their traditional homeland became the Yaquis' unique way of life. The genius of this indigenous people lay in working out a new arrangement acceptable both to themselves and to the Spaniards. Yaquis understood implicitly what Jesuits had adamantly refused to accept: that their survival as a distinct people and culture depended most crucially upon their willingness to help develop the local Spanish economy, which meant supplying manpower for the mines. Only by such a compromise were they able to blunt efforts at integrating them more forcefully and completely into the larger colonial society, whose rigid hierarchy would have relegated them to the lowest rungs. In other words, while bowing to demands for their labor, their simultaneous insistence on cultural separatism and political autonomy signalled their refusal to be assimilated into the yori society.

Notes

Chapter 2

[1]The pioneer works in identifying the indigenous nations are by Mexican scholars: Manuel Orozco y Berra, *Geografía de las lenguas y carta etnográfica de México* (Mexico: Impr. de J. M. Andrade y F. Escalante, 1864); Fernando Pimentel, *Cuadro descriptivo y comparativo de las lenguas indígenas de México,* 3 vols. (Mexico: Tip. de I. Epstein, 1874–75). These have been followed by several North American studies: Cyrus Thomas, *Indian Languages of Mexico and Central America and Their Geographical Distribution* (Washington, D.C.: Government Printing Office, 1911); Clark Wissler, *The American Indian, An Introduction to the Anthropology of the New World* (New York: D. C. McMurtrie, 1917); A. L. Kroeber, *Cultural and Natural Areas of Native North America* (Berkeley: University of California Press, 1939).

The most definitive and precise studies in the Mexican northwest are two works by Carl O. Sauer: *The Distribution of Aboriginal Tribes and Languages in Northwestern Mexico,* Ibero-Americana, no. 5 (Berkeley: University of California Press, 1934) and *The Aboriginal Population of Northwest Mexico,* Ibero-Americana, no. 10 (Berkeley: University of California Press, 1935). More recently, the noted anthropologist Edward Spicer has added new organizational insights into the complicated problem of identifying and locating the numerous aboriginal nations of the "Greater Southwest," in *Cycles of Conquest* (Tucson: University of Arizona Press, 1962). The absence of concrete, pre-Hispanic records on the great diversity of cultures and languages has made it extremely difficult for scholars to identify and determine the distribution and size of the indigenous peoples of the Mexican northwest.

For a detailed, rather technical discussion of the geography of present-day southern Arizona, Sonora, and the northern tip of Sinaloa, *see* Roger Dunbier, *The Sonoran Desert* (Tucson: University of Arizona Press, 1968). Paul Kirchhoff has dubbed the river-flooded parts of the Mexican northwest an "oasis America" within larger Arid America, in "Gatherers and Farmers in the Greater Southwest," *American Anthropologist*, n.s., 56 (August 1954): 533; *see* map on p. 544.

²Kirchhoff, "Gatherers and Farmers," p. 533. In addition to the works cited in note 1 above, the following also deal in detail with languages: A. L. Kroeber, *Uto-Aztecan Languages of Mexico*, Ibero-Americana, no. 8 (Berkeley: University of California Press, 1934); Ralph L. Beals, *The Aboriginal Culture of the Cáhita Indians*, Ibero-Americana, no. 19 (Berkeley: University of California Press, 1943); Ralph L. Beals, *The Contemporary Culture of the Cáhita Indians* (Washington, D.C.: The Smithsonian Institution Bureau of American Ethnology, 1945).

³The discussion is based on Sauer, *Distribution*, and Sauer, *Aboriginal Population*. *See* Spicer, *Cycles*, for more detailed historical and ethnological summaries of the Seris, Navajos, and Apaches; on p. 23 is a chart comparing the tribal names used in historical writings and by members of the tribes. *See also* the *Handbook of Middle American Indians*, vol. 8, *Ethnology*, p. 2 (Austin: University of Texas Press, 1969).

⁴Discussion of the Opatas and Pimas is based on Spicer, *Cycles; Handbook*, vol. 8; Sauer, *Distribution;* and Sauer, *Aboriginal Population.*

⁵The most widely cited and accepted estimate of the original Yaqui population was made by Andrés Pérez de Ribas, *Historia de los triunfos de N. S. Fe entre gentes las más bárbaras y fieras del Nuevo Orbe,* 3 vols. (Mexico: Ed. Layac, 1944), 2:64. Pérez de Ribas was the first Jesuit missionary in the Yaqui. His career will be discussed more fully in Chapter Three.

⁶Edward Spicer, *Perspectives in American Indian Culture Change* (Chicago: University of Chicago Press, 1961), pp. 12, 14. Although there is no information on the aboriginal Yaqui family structure, based on existing kinship terminology, Beals has postulated the theory of the bilateral family. Beals, *Aboriginal Culture*, p. 52.

⁷Carlos Basauri, *La población indígena de México, Etnografía* (Mexico: Sría. de Educ. Pub., 1940), p. 246; Spicer, *Perspectives*, p. 13; Pérez de Ribas, *Triunfos* 2: 10.

⁸Pérez de Ribas, *Triunfos* 2: 64; Beals, *Aboriginal Culture*, pp. 11–12.

⁹Miguel Othón de Mendizábal, "La evolución del noroeste de México," in *Obras Completas*, vol. 2 (Mexico: 1964), pp. 38–39; Spicer, *Perspectives*, p. 12; Beals, *Aboriginal Culture*, pp. 11–12.

[10]Beals, *Aboriginal Culture*, pp. 21–37.

[11]Beals, *Aboriginal Culture*, p. 40; Mendizábal, "Evolución," p. 38; Spicer, *Perspectives*, p. 16.

[12]Pérez de Ribas, *Triunfos* 2: 76–83.

[13]Pérez de Ribas, *Triunfos* 2: 63–146 passim, is full of descriptions of Yaqui ceremonies and celebrations, especially concerning war and peace. Another beautiful description of a Yaqui hunting ceremony can be found in George P. Hammond and Agapito Rey, *Obregón's History of Sixteenth Century Explorations in Western America* (Los Angeles: Wetzel Pub. Co., 1929), p. 259.

[14]Beals, *Aboriginal Culture*, pp. 60, 66; Spicer, *Perspectives*, p. 16.

[15]Beals, *Aboriginal Culture*, pp. 61–62; Spicer, *Perspectives*, p. 17; Mendizábal, "Evolución," p. 38; *see* Mendizábal pp. 62–65 for a discussion of totemism. Cabeza de Vaca safely passed through a large tract of Indian territory because he and his companions had established a reputation as healers; they were probably regarded as some sort of *hechicero*, or shaman. *See* pp. 16–17 of chapter 2 for a brief historical discussion of Cabeza de Vaca.

[16]Mendizábal, "Evolución," p. 53.

[17]For a resume of Cortés's activities in the northwest, *see* Hubert Howe Bancroft, *Works*, vol. 15, *History of the North American States and Texas, 1531–1800* (San Francisco: A. L. Bancroft, 1884), pp. 40–70.

[18]For a resumé of Nuño de Guzmán's activities in the northwest, *see* Bancroft, *Works* 15: 26–70. For the history of Nueva Galicia, *see* Alonso de la Mota y Escobar's work, written around 1600: *Descripción geográfica de los reinos de Nueva Galicia, Nueva Vizcaya y Nuevo León* (Mexico: Robredo, 1940); Antonio Tello, "Fragmentos de una historia de la Nueva Galicia, escrita hacia 1650," in Joaquín García Icazbalceta, *Colección de documentos para la historia de México*, vol. 2 (Mexico: Antigua Librería, 1866), pp. 343–438; Matías de la Mota Padilla, *Historia de la conquista de la provincia de la Nueva Galicia en 1742* (Mexico: Impr. del Gobierno, 1870); José López-Portillo y Weber, *La rebelión de Nueva Galicia* (Mexico: Inst. Panam. Geog. e Hist., 1938). These works by no means exhaust the literature on Nueva Galicia but are some of the more important ones.

[19]"Segunda relación anónima de la jornada que hizo Nuño de Guzmán de la Nueva Galicia," in Icazbalceta, *Colección* 2: 296–306; "Proceso del Marquéz del Valle y Nuño de Guzmán y los adelantados Soto y Alvarado, sobre el descubrimiento de la Tierra Nueva (Año de 1541)," in *Colección de documentos inéditos relativos al descubrimiento, conquista y organización de las antiguas posesiones españoles de América y Oceanía, sacados de los archivos del de Indias*, vol. 15 (Madrid: Impr. de José María Pérez, 1871), pp. 300–408. Diego de Guzmán's report, entitled "Relación de lo que yo Diego de Guzmán he descobrieto en la costa de la Mar del Sur por Su Magestad y por el Ilustre Señor Nuño de Guzmán, Gobernador de la Nueva Galicia," is included among the many documents reproduced in "Proceso del Marquéz del Valle," in *Colección de documentos inéditas* 15: 325–38.

[20]Andrés Alonso's notarial record of this event, dated 4 October 1533, is included in "Proceso del Marquéz del Valle," in *Colección de documentos inéditas* 15: 324–25.

[21]"Segunda relación anónima," in Icazbalceta, *Colección* 2: 201–4.

²²The *relación,* or report, of Alvar Núñez Cabeza de Vaca, first published in 1542, has been translated into English and edited by two persons: Buckingham Smith, trans., *Relation of Alvar Núñez Cabeza de Vaca* (New York: n.p., 1871) and Fanny Bandelier, trans., *The Journey of Alvar Núñez Cabeza de Vaca And His Companions from Florida to the Pacific, 1528–1536* (New York: A. S. Barnes, 1905).

²³Translation by Bandelier, *Journey,* pp. 161–62, 166.

²⁴George F. Winship, "The Coronado Expedition, 1540–42," *14th Annual Report of the Bureau of Ethnology,* pt. 1 (Washington, D.C.: 1896), pp. 339–615. This work includes the original Spanish and an English translation of Pedro Castañeda's *Narrative.* For a more popularly written account of Coronado, *see* Herbert E. Bolton, *Coronado, Knight of Pueblos and Plains* (Albuquerque: University of New Mexico Press, 1949). For two particularly readable histories of the various expeditions in search of Cíbola, Quivira, and other mythical kingdoms rich in gold, *see* Adolph F. Bandelier, *The Gilded Man* (New York: Appleton, 1893) and Carl O. Sauer, *The Road to Cíbola,* Ibero-Americana, no. 3 (Berkeley: University of California Press, 1932).

One of Cabeza de Vaca's companions, the black Moorish slave Estevánico, accompanied the Franciscan friar, Marcos de Niza, on the next expedition in search of Cíbola in 1539. At one time they must have crossed the Yaqui River, but left no record of it. Friar Niza's claim of having actually sighted the fabulous cities of Cíbola was typical of the exaggerations of Spanish explorers of this time.

²⁵For a history of Francisco de Ibarra, *see* J. Lloyd Mecham, *Francisco de Ibarra and Nueva Vizcaya* (Durham, N.C.: Duke University Press, 1927). *See also* Atanasio G. Saravia, *Apuntes para la historia de la Nueva Vizcaya* (Mexico: Impr. Reveles, 1928) and "Relación de los descubrimientos conquistas y poblaciones hechas por el gobernador Francisco de Ibarra en las provincias de Copala, Nueva Vizcaya y Chiametla (Año de 1554)," in *Colección de documentos inéditas* 4: 463–84.

²⁶This summary and the quotes are from Hammond, *Obregón's History,* pp. 257–60.

²⁷Bancroft, *Works* 15: 113–15; Luis Navarro García, *Sonora y Sinaloa en el siglo XVII* (Sevilla: Escuela de Estudios Hispano-Americanos, 1967), p. 161.

²⁸Mota y Escobar, *Descripción geográfica,* pp. 211–18.

Chapter 3

¹For a succinct history of the founding of the Jesuits and their introduction to New Spain, *see* Jerome V. Jacobsen, "Pedro Sánchez, Founder of the Jesuits in New Spain," *Mid-America* 22 (July 1940): 157–90. The history of the Jesuit order in New Spain and especially in the northwest where they had the greatest success as missionaries has been written by Jesuit historians since the seventeenth century. This is not surprising since they alone had access to all the important missionary documents. The first history of the Jesuit missionaries in the northwest was Andrés Pérez de Ribas, *Triunfos,* first published in 1645. The same author followed with a second work, *Crónica y historia relativa de la provincia de la Compañía de Jesús en Nueva España* (Mexico: Impr. del Sagrada Corazón de Jesús,

1896); for some reason, this work is far less accessible than the first. Two other works written by later Jesuit historians are important: Gerardo Decorme, *La obra de los Jesuitas mexicanos durante la época colonial, 1572–1767,* vol. 2, *Las misiones* (Mexico: Antigua Lib. Robredo de J. Porrúa e Hijos, 1941) and Francisco Javier Alegre, *Historia de la Provinica de la Compañía de Jesús de Nueva España,* new ed. by Ernest J. Burrus and Feliz Zubillaga, 4 vols. (Rome: Inst. Histo. S. J., 1956). Herbert E. Bolton was the secular American historian who had done the most extensive work on the Jesuit missions in the north of Mexico and had trained a large group of historians at the University of California at Berkeley, most of whom were Jesuits, to continue his work. Jacobsen, Dunne, Bannon, and Shiels are several of Bolton's Jesuit students whose works are citied in this study. Another work of some importance is Manuel Orozco y Berra, *Historia de la dominación española en México,* vol. 3, Biblioteca Histórica Mexicana de Obras Inéditas, no. 10 (Mexico: Porrúa, 1938).

The Bancroft Library of the University of California at Berkeley has collected originals or copies of many important Jesuit documents, e.g., the *cartas anuas,* or annual reports, from the missions. These are contained in bound volumes entitled: "Memorias para la historica de Sinaloa," and "Documentos para la historia de Sinaloa."

For the history of the early Jesuit activities in Mexico City, *see* Jerome V. Jacobsen, *Educational Foundations of the Jesuits in 16th Century New Spain* (Berkeley: University of California Press, 1938).

[2] For the history of Franciscan missionaries in Nueva Vizcaya, *see* José Arlegui, *Crónica de la Provincia de N.S.P.S. Francisco de Zacatecas* Mexico: n.p., 1737).

[3] Decorme, *Obra,* p. viii.

[4] Herbert E. Bolton, "The Mission as a Frontier Institution in the Spanish American Colonies," *American Historical Review* 23 (October 1917): 45.

[5] An excellent institutional study of the northwest missions is the work by Jesuit Father Charles W. Polzer, *Rules and Precepts of the Jesuit Missions of Northwestern New Spain* (Tucson: University of Arizona Press, 1976). The book contains translations of a number of important Jesuit documents dealing with these missions.

[6] Mendizábal, "Evolución," p. 63. Raul Flores Guerrero, "El imperialismo jesuita en la Nueva España," *Historia Mexicana* 4 (October–December 1954): 166.

[7] Mendizábal, "Evolución," has an especially interesting discussion of the Jesuit operational plan and a comparison of the indigenous culture of the north with that of the Aztecs.

[8] For a biography of Father Tapia, who led the first contingent of Jesuits to Sinaloa, *see* William E. Shiels, *Gonzalo de Tapia (1561–1595),* U.S. Catholic Historical Society Monograph Series, no. 4 (New York: 1934). For a short biography of Captain Hurdaide, *see* Harry P. Johnson, "Diego Martínez de Hurdaide, Defender of Spain's Pacific Coast Frontier," in *Greater America, Essays in Honor of Herbert Eugene Bolton* (Berkeley: University of California Press, 1945), pp. 199–218.

[9] Bancroft, *Works* 15: 213. The figures are from the carta anua of 1604, which

reported 10,000 souls converted in that year alone. At the end of the sixteenth century, the Jesuits had only 10,000 conversions, according to Mendizábal, "Evolución," p. 55, citing a Jesuit source. If these figures are correct, the process of conversion sped up considerably during the first years of the seventeenth century.

[10]Decorme, *Obra,* p. 315, n. 1, from carta anua of 1613. Father Velasco's grammar has been discovered and printed in Eustaquio Buelna, *Arte de la lengua cáhita, por un padre de la Compañía de Jesús* (Mexico: Impr. del Gobierno, 1891).

[11]Decorme, *Obra,* p. 324, records 1608 as the date of Hurdaide's first advance to the Yaqui. Pérez de Ribas, *Triunfos* 2: 66–75, the main source for these events, does not provide a clear chronological guide, but he was an eyewitness. The carta anua of 1610 also gives some details of these events; a copy of this document can be found in "Documentos para la historia de Sinaloa," vol. 1. Bancroft Library, University of Californa, Berkeley, California.

Alegre, *Historia* 2: 204, identifies another rebel leader, Babilonio, as a cacique from the Fuerte (Suaqui) mission. Pérez de Ribas first used the term *cacique* to denote whomever he perceived to be a leader, chief, or headman according to the usage established by Spaniards. It was not, of course, a Yaqui word and did not subsequently gain widespread currency in the northwest.

[12]Pérez de Ribas, *Triunfos* 2: 76–82. Several letters of Hurdaide, extracted in Johnson, "Hurdaide," contain additional information on these events.

[13]Alegre, *Historia* 2: 210.

[14]Hurdaide's letter, reproduced in part in Alegre, *Historia* 2: 253–54; Pérez de Ribas, *Triunfos* 2: 14–15.

[15]Pérez de Ribas, *Triunfos* 2: 13–24, reproduces some of Father Méndez's letters from the Mayo mission. Méndez's letters were also included in the carta anua of 1614, included in "Documentos para la historia de Sinaloa," vol. 1. Bancroft Library, University of California, Berkeley, California.

[16]Peter M. Dunne, *Pioneer Jesuits in Northern Mexico* (Berkeley: University of California Press, 1944), pp. 41–44, 119–21, 162. The Tepehuan mission and rebellion have been studied at some length by Jesuit historians. In addition to Dunne, who provides a detailed, if somewhat biased, account, *see* Decorme, *Obra,* pp. 56–76; Alegre, *Historia* 2: 270–308. There is also an important secular report on the rebellion, entitled "Relación breve y sucinta de los sucesos que ha tenido la guerra de los Tepehuanes de la Nueva Vizcaya desde 15 de noviembre de 1616 hasta 16 de mayo de 1618," in Charles W. Hackett, ed., *Historical Documents Relating to New Mexico, Nueva Vizcaya and Approaches Thereto,* collected by A. Bandelier and Fanny R. Bandelier, 3 vols. (Washington, D.C.: Carnegie Institute, 1923), 2: 100–13. This document is reproduced in the original Spanish with a facing English translation.

The rebellion was finally suppressed in May 1617, when Governor Gaspar de Alvear of Nueva Vizcaya mobilized all the Spaniards and numerous Indian allies for a campaign. He concentrated his efforts on capturing the hechicero-turned-rebel-chief Gogoxito. Throughout the pacification campaign, his treatment of captured rebels was insatiably cruel. Goaded by an uncontrollable furor to avenge the losses suffered by the Spanish population, he literally scourged the countryside for 600 miles, burning all crops and Indian settlements in sight.

[17]Dunne, *Pioneer Jesuits,* p. 51. According to Dunne, the Tepehuanes tried to seduce Yaquis with looted objects from the Tepehuan mission churches.

[18]Father Basilio learned the Yaqui language so well in his years among the Yaquis that he has been credited with the authorship of the "Arte e catechismo de la lengua cáhita," in Buelna, *Arte de la lengua cáhita.*

[19]Pérez de Ribas, *Triunfos* 2: 87–88. Pérez de Ribas, himself a participant, has provided the definitive account of the first Jesuit entry into the Yaqui in 1617. All other versions are based on this source. Unfortunately, he wrote many years after his experience in the Yaqui; consequently, many retrospective thoughts have intermingled with recollection of his first impressions. Also lamentable for the historian was his almost total omission of dates and statistics.

[20]Pérez de Ribas, *Triunfos* 2: 91–93.

[21]Pérez de Ribas, *Triunfos* 2: 96–97. At this point, Pérez de Ribas's memoirs appear especially disjointed and garbled, stringing together disparate pieces of information without any apparent thematic or chronological coherence. He is imbued with his own missionary zeal in the most intense spiritual sense, which is, unfortunately, not always useful to the historian. Beyond the activities of the first few days, it becomes an increasingly frustrating task to sort out what took place and when, even during his own three-year tenure in the mission. This vagueness helps explain the disparities in later versions of the founding of the Yaqui mission, not to mention the huge gaps or total lack of information on several important aspects of the mission system.

[22]Pérez de Ribas, *Triunfos* 2: 163.

[23]Pérez de Ribas, *Triunfos* 2: 118–21. Apparently, the Jesuits were never able to eradicate totally the presence or influence of hechiceros and eventually learned to tolerate them. On the other hand, missionaries early on gained the upper hand over these "tribal magicians." Polzer, *Rules,* pp. 44–45. According to Polzer, the tolerance began to break down towards the closing years of the Jesuit era. Also, presumably Carlos Castañeda's Don Juan (*see* Bibliography), the Yaqui "witch," is a modern day hechicero, if indeed he actually exists.

[24]Pérez de Ribas, *Triunfos* 2: 18–19.

[25]Pérez de Ribas, *Triunfos* 2: 80–120 passim. The use of converted individuals or even families from other nations in new missions was a common practice established by the missionaries. Just as the missionized Indians served the Spaniards as auxiliaries in the military campaigns, so they served the fathers as apostolic assistants. In both these activities and later as colonists, the Yaquis played a substantial role. It was very rare that Jesuits brought Spaniards into a mission to serve as good moral examples.

[26]Decorme, *Obra,* p. 330; Alegre, *Historia* 2: 327.

[27]Alegre, *Historia* 2: 325; Decorme, *Obra,* p. 330. Both Jesuit historians give the date as 1620. As Pérez de Ribas provides no date when he mentions this event, this probably explains the discrepancy among sources.

[28]Pérez de Ribas, *Triunfos* 2: 112. Again, he provides no specific date, except to

claim that two years after the arrival of Father Villalta, all 30,000 Yaquis were baptized. The carta anua of 1624 provides a specific breakdown of baptized Yaquis, according to resident missionary:

Father Pedro Méndez	7,250
Father Juan Ardeñas (Cardenas?)	4,000
Father Guillermo Ottón (Oten?)	3,800
	15,050

For some unexplained reason, Father Tomás Basilio, who was definitely still operating in the Yaqui mission, was left out of this list. This omission was corrected the following year, 1625, in a comprehensive census of all Jesuit missions in Nueva Vizcaya. Unfortunately, the list was ordered by names of missionaries alone, without reference to their mission or station post. Based on what is known, the following missionaries, grouped together in the 1625 census list, worked in the Yaqui at this time:

Father Pedro Méndez	7,250
Father Juan de Cardenas (Ardeñas?)	4,000
Father Tomás Basilio	5,400
Father Guillermo Oten (Ottón?)	3,800
	20,450

Despite the discrepancies in spelling for the names Cardenas, or Ardeñas, and Oten, or Ottón, the figures given by their names on both lists are exactly the same. With the addition of Father Basilio in 1625, the revised list appears complete, giving the total Yaqui population at 20,450. This figure still falls short of the 30,000 consistently cited by Pérez de Ribas. There are some possible explanations for the apparent discrepancy, none of which can be confirmed. One, Pérez de Ribas's estimate was greatly exaggerated, when a substantial number of Indians had managed to escape baptism and the mission system. Two, and this seem more likely, the 20,450 figure included only baptized adults, leaving out children under seven who were baptized without prior doctrinal education, as was Jesuit custom.

For the 1625 census, *see* "Razón y minuta de los indios que se administran en las provincias de la Nueva Vizcaya por los vicarios beneficiados y religiosos de San Francisco y Compañía de Jesus que hoy están bautizados (1625)," in Hackett, *Historical Documents* 2:152–55. Part of the carta anua of 1624 is copied in Peter M. Dunne, *Pioneer Black Robes on the West Coast* (Berkeley: University of California Press, 1940), app. 1, p. 217.

[29]Again, Pérez de Ribas gives no date; consequently Decorme and Alegre have also not assigned one. Obviously, the process took many years. By some way, Roberto Acosta ascertained that the reduction was completed around 1623; *see* his *Apuntes históricos sonorenses. La conquista temporal y espiritual del Yaqui y el Mayo* (Mexico: Impr. Aldina, 1949), p. 63.

[30]María Elena Galavíz de Capdevielle, *Rebeliones indígenas en el norte del Reino de la Nueva España XVI–XVIII* (Mexico: Ed. Campesina, 1967), p. 57.Other authors have presented other versions of the Yaqui creation myth. According to Basauri, *Población indígena,* p. 264, a tribe of tall people lived in the Yaqui Valley and another tribe of small people lived in the sierra. In the twelfth century,

catastrophe and disaster drove the small people from the sierra to the valley; the two peoples mixed and the Yaqui nation resulted. Another interesting myth is presented by Fortunato Hernández: the Yaquis were actually Toltecs, who, when harassed by Apaches and other tribes, left the city of Tlapallan on the Gila or Colorado River in the year 544. After eight years of wandering, they arrived at their present location in Sinaloa and defeated the inferior tribes who were already there. This last version is least credible and sounds vaguely like the Aztec myth of creation. See Hernández, *Las razas indígenas de Sonora y las guerras del Yaqui* (Mexico: Casa Edit. J. de Elizaldo, 1902), p. 108.

[31]Pérez de Ribas never once gave the full names of the eight Yaqui mission pueblos nor of the eleven earlier reductions along the river. The complete names can be found in Acosta, *Apuntes históricos*, p. 63, and Juan Ortíz Zapata, "Relación de las misiones que la Compañía de Jesús tiene en el reino y provincia de la Nueva Vizcaya en la Nueva España, hecha el año de 1678...," in *Documentos para la historia de México*, ser. 4, vol. 3 (Mexico: published for Manuel Orozco y Berra, 1907), pp. 301–419. This is a twenty-volume collection of important colonial documents arranged in four series, published by Manuel Orozco y Berra and indexed by Genaro García. There is some discrepancy between Acosta and Zapata on the first parts of the names, which only suggests how seldomly used the cumbersome full names are. Usually only the last parts are used, and these are consistent in all sources. I have standardized the spellings according to present day usage.

[32]Pérez de Ribas, *Triunfos* 2: 126.

[33]Spicer, *Perspectives*, p. 23; Joseph Och, *Missionary in Sonora, 1755–1767,* trans. from the German by Theodore E. Treutlein (San Francisco: California Historical Society, 1965), p. 151.

[34]Pérez de Ribas provides little systematic information on this aspect. Other Jesuits who had labored among the Yaquis also left no record. Fortunately, in the eighteenth century, several German Jesuits (Och, cited above, and Pfefferkorn, cited below) working in the Sonora missions were extremely prolific writers. Although they also left many important areas unsatisfactorily covered, they have provided many more details about the mission system than Pérez de Ribas did. Going on the rather safe assumption that Jesuits followed the same blueprint in founding missions in the northwest and because there is no other source of information, it has been necessary to borrow liberally from Och, Pfefferkorn, and Nentuig, cited below.

In the eighteenth century, because of the shortage of Spanish personnel, the Crown revised its policy to allow foreign, or non-Spanish, Jesuits to work in New Spain. Many of these foreign Jesuits were German-speakers. Dunne describes these German missionaries as "as a rule more observant and realistic, and also less charitable than Latins" towards both Indians and secular colonial officials; *Juan Antonio Balthasar, Padre Visitador to the Sonoran Frontier, 1744–1745* (Tucson: Arizona Pioneers' Historical Society, 1957), p. 30.

[35]Ignaz Pfefferkorn, *Sonora. A Description of the Province,* trans. and annotated by Theodore E. Treutlein (Albuquerque: University of New Mexico Press, 1949), p. 266.

[36]Spicer, *Perspectives,* p. 33. The Yaquis have incorporated the Spanish word *gobernador* into their own language as *kobanao*. There are other examples of such

incorporations; *see* William Kurath and Edward Spicer, *A Brief Introduction to Yaqui. A Native Language of Sonora,* University of Arizona Bulletin, vol. 18, no. 1, Social Science Bulletin, no. 15 (Tucson: University of Arizona, 1947). A more serious linguistic study is Jean B. Johnson, *El idioma yaqui* (Mexico: Inst. Nac. de Antrop. e Hist., 1962).

[37]Pfefferkorn, *Sonora,* p. 266. In the Archivo General de la Nación de México (AGNM), Ramo de Historia 16: 8–137, there is an ostensibly anonymous and important document entitled: "Descripción geográfica natural y curiosa de la Provincia de Sonora, por un Amigo del Servicio de Díos; y del Rey Nuestro Señor. Año de 1764." This same document appears again in AGNM Historia 383 and in *Documentos para la historia de México,* ser. 3, vol. 1: 489–637. This same document also surfaced under a slightly different title: "Rudo Ensayo, tentative de una prevención al descripción geográfica de la Provincia de Sonora, sus términos y confines,... por un amigo del buen común, 1763"; this is the version translated and published in English as: *Rudo Ensayo By An Unknown Jesuit Padre, 1763,* trans. by Eusebio Guiteras, *Records of the American Catholic Historical Society of Philadelphia,* vol. 5, no. 2 (1894) and reissued by Arizona Silhouettes (Tucson: 1951). Scholars have determined that this document was the work of Jesuit Father Juan Nentuig; *see* Albert F. Pradeau, "Descripción de Sonora del Padre Nentuig," in *Archivo General de la Nación de México. Boletin,* vol. 26, no. 2 (1935): 239–53. Father Nentuig made many observations similar to those of Och and Pfefferkorn, and these three works complement each other. Citations from Nentuig are taken from the English *Rudo Ensayo,* which is the most legible version; much of the reproduction in AGNM Historia and Documentos are not easily readable.

The Anonymous Reporter of the Diego de Guzmán expedition first noticed the staff carried by the leader of the Yaqui warriors. "Segunda relación anónima," in Icazbalceta, *Colección* 2: 296–306; *see also* Och, *Missionary,* p. 167.

[38]Och, *Missionary,* p. 167.

[39]Pfefferkorn, *Sonora,* p. 266; Och, *Missionary,* p. 167; Nentuig, *Rudo Ensayo,* p. 123.

[40]Pérez de Ribas, *Triunfos* 2: 126.

[41]Pfefferkorn, *Sonora,* p. 266; Och, *Missionary,* p. 167.

[42]Pfefferkorn, *Sonora,* p. 267; Nentuig, *Rudo Ensayo,* p. 122.

[43]Pérez de Ribas, *Triunfos* 2: 127.

[44]Pérez de Ribas, *Triunfos* 2: 126; Pfefferkorn, *Sonora,* p. 267.

[45]Nentuig, *Rudo Ensayo,* p. 123; Och, *Missionary,* p. 167.

[46]Pérez de Ribas, *Triunfos* 2: 63–145 passim, makes several passing references to Yaqui musical instruments and talents; *see,* for example, his description on p. 122.

In the words of Jesuit historian Decorme, "to teach them Spanish was to encourage their disintegration and perdition, as it is well known what kind of Christian life they could have led in the mines and as peons in the ranches. If this state of things favored the public prosperity and the fusion of races, it certainly acted to the detriment of the intellectual, moral and religious character of the poor Indian...." *Obra,* p. xvii.

[47]Mendizábal, "Evolución," p. 63.

[48]If Pérez de Ribas unsatisfactorily described the political and social reorganization of the mission, he was even more so regarding economic reorganization. Again, it is necessary to resort to the German Jesuits and their experiences in Sonora: Pfefferkorn, *Sonora,* pp. 274–75; also Nentuig, *Rudo Ensayo,* pp. 123–24. Theodore E. Treutlein, translator of Och and Pfefferkorn, has synthesized Pfefferkorn's observations on the economic aspect of the mission in an article: "The Economic Regime of the Jesuit Mission in Eighteenth Century Sonora," *Pacific Historical Review* 8 (September 1939): 289–300. At least one modern Jesuit historian, John Bannon, in his article, "Pioneer Jesuit Missionaries on the Pacific Slope of New Spain" *Greater America,* pp. 181–97, has lamented the paucity of information on the economic aspect of the mission. Pérez de Ribas, *Triunfos* 2: 64, provides a brief, but valuable, observation on the Yaquis' agricultural activities and conditions when he first arrived.

[49]Nentuig, *Rudo Ensayo,* p. 123; Treutlein, "Economic Regime," p. 292.

[50]Bannon, "Pioneer Jesuit Missionaries," p. 195.

[51]Spicer, *Perspectives,* p. 24; Bannon, "Pioneer," p. 194; Nentuig, *Rudo Ensayo,* p. 124.

[52]Bannon, "Pioneer," p. 195. Nentuig, *Rudo Ensayo,* p. 27, notes that while Sonora was very suitable to cattle ranching, the frequent Apache raids had destroyed many of the ranches. Since the Apaches did not penetrate as far south as the Yaqui mission after the middle of the eighteenth century, presumably the ranches in southern Sonora and Sinaloa were able to flourish.

[53]Pfefferkorn, *Sonora,* p. 275; Nentuig, *Rudo Ensayo,* p. 124.

[54]Pfefferkorn, *Sonora,* pp. 275–76.

[55]Pérez de Ribas, *Crónica,* pp. 527–29, describes how Father Zambrano of Santa Cruz del Mayo had to follow his Indian charges to the mountains during a famine in 1622.

[56]"Apologético defensorio y puntual manifiesto que los Padres de la Compañía de Jesús, misioneros de las Provincias de Zinaloa y Zonora, ofrecen por noviembre de este año de 1657, al Rectísimo Tribunal y Senador Justísimo de la Razón, de la Equidad y de la Justicia, contra las antiguas, presentes y futuras calumnias, que les ha forjado la envidia, les fabrica la malevolencia y cada día les está maquinando la iniquidad." A copy of the original is in AGNM Historia 316: 359–425, reproduced in large part in Pablo Herrera Carillo, "Sinaloa a mediados del siglo XVII," *Congreso Mexicano de Historia, Memorias y Revistas* (Mexico: 1960), pp. 145–74. This citation is from Herrera Carrillo, p. 172. Dunne attributes authorship of this document to Father Francisco Paría, who was not known to have been a missionary in the northwest; *Juan Antonio Balthasar,* p. 62.

[57]Acosta, *Apuntes históricos,* pp. 78–79.

[58]Pfefferkorn, *Sonora,* p. 284. For an excellent discussion of the political and social conditions of Nueva Vizcaya in the late seventeenth century, *see* the Introduction to Hackett, *Historical Documents,* vol. 2.

[59]The Marín reports are discussed in the Introduction to Hackett, *Historical Documents* 2: 15. The full reports are reproduced in this volume as: "Testimonio de cartas y informes del Campo Don Joseph Francisco Marín (3 de agosto hasta

30 de septiembre de 1693)," pp. 364–409. A listing of the Indian nations in Nueva Vizcaya is found on pp. 392–95.

[60]"Al gobernador de la Nueva Vizcaya guarde las cédulas que están dados, para que no se hagan esclavos a los indios y los conserven en paz quietud y justicia (Madrid, 30 de noviembre de 1647)," in Hackett, *Historical Documents* 2: 161–63.

[61]"Apologético defensorio," Herrera Carrillo, pp. 127, 149–50. This and all subsequent citations from the same document are taken from the published version in Herrera Carrillo, *see* note 56 above.

[62]"Apologético defensorio," p. 155. On Perea, *see* note 71 below.

[63]"Apologético defensorio," p. 157. Actually, at this time several mines werebeing worked in Copala and Rosario, in southern Sinaloa. Navarro García, *Sonora y Sinaloa*, p. 214.

[64]"Apologético defensorio," p. 161.

[65]Pfefferkorn, *Sonora*, p. 278.

[66]"Apologético defensorio," p. 161.

[67]Pérez de Ribas, *Triunfos* 2: 217. Robert West mentions Indians from Sinaloa and Sonora working the Parral mines in the early seventeenth century; *The Mining Community in Northern New Spain: The Parral Mining District,* Ibero-Americana, no. 30 (Berkeley: University of California Press, 1949), p. 64.

[68]The major documents of this matter are reproduced in the section entitled: "Autos which came with letters from the Viceroy, dated February 28, 1639, concerning whether the division of bishoprics in New Mexico and doctrinas of Sinaloa would be desirable," in Hackett, *Historical Documents* 3: 94–127 (Unlike vols. 1 and 2, vol. 3 no longer contains the Spanish originals). There is also a photographic reproduction of an original letter by the Bishop of Nueva Vizcaya regarding this matter, entitled: "Informe cerca de las misiones que tiene la Provincia de la Religión de la Compañía de Jesús de México en el Reino de Nueva Vizcaya por el obispo y teniente de gobernador de aquel distrito (5 de mayo, 1638)," in Alegre, *Historia* 2, app. XXI–B, between pp. 522–23.

[69]Andrés Pérez de Ribas, "Petition" (of Father Andrés Pérez de Ribas and other chaplains of the Company of Jesus, College of Mexico, September 12, 1638), in Hackett, *Historical Documents* 3: 95–105. The Spanish original can be found in Alegre, *Historia* 2: 581–94, app. XXI–B.

[70]Pérez de Ribas, "Petition," p. 102.

[71]Pérez de Ribas, *Triunfos* 2: 127. From 1640 to 1645, the Jesuits successfully withstood another challenge. Pedro de Perea, Captain of Sinaloa and successor to Hurdaide, created the kingdom of Nueva Andalucia out of Sonora, called in Franciscan missionaries, who actually arrived, to administer to the Optas and Pimas, and also brought in 150 Spanish colonists. But with his death in 1645, the legitimacy of Nueva Andalucia was rescinded and the Jesuits regained hegemony over the Indians of Sonora. *See* Navarro García, *Sonora y Sinaloa*, pp. 249–54.

[72]This was the important document, "Apologético defensorio." *See* note 56 above.

[73]Navarro García, *Sonora y Sinaloa*, pp. 37–38.

[74]Navarro García, *Sonora y Sinaloa,* pp. 39–40; Acosta, *Apuntes históricos,* pp. 75–77. There is a description of Alamos in Francisco Javier de Gamboa, *Comentarios a las Ordenanzas de Minas* (Madrid: Oficina de Joaquín Ibarra, 1761), p. 502: "...en el principio de este siglo era el mineral mas abundante de plata...." Father Eusebio Kino was also eyewitness to the flourishing of the Alamos mines; for his impressions, *see* Herbert E. Bolton, *Rim of Christendom. A Biography of Eusebio Francisco Kino* (New York: Macmillan Co., 1936).

[75]Navarro García, *Sonora y Sinaloa,* p. 38.

[76]West, *Mining Community,* pp. 47–49. Pérez de Ribas, "Petition."

[77]Navarro García, *Sonora y Sinaloa,* pp. 175–88. This conflict which began in 1672 is presented in great detail on pp. 175–234.

[78]Navarro García, *Sonora y Sinaloa,* p. 176.

[79]Navarro García, *Sonora y Sinaloa,* pp. 178–79.

[80]Navarro García, *Sonora y Sinaloa,* p. 182. Although the judge was decidedly anti-Jesuit, he appointed the commission so that the Jesuits could not accuse him later of unfairness. He had in mind specifically the conflicts between Jesuits and civil authorities in Paraguay.

[81]Haro y Monterrosos, quoted in Navarro García, *Sonora y Sinaloa,* p. 182.

[82]Navarro García, *Sonora y Sinaloa,* pp. 187, 192, 195–96.

[83]Navarro García, *Sonora y Sinaloa,* pp. 206–07; Salcedo quoted on p. 205.

[84]For an excellent discussion of the *Obedesco pero no cumplo* and other administrative concepts, *see* John Phelan, "Authority and Flexibility in the Spanish Imperial Bureaucracy," *Administrative Science Quarterly* 5 (1940): 47–65.

[85]Navarro García, *Sonora y Sinaloa,* pp. 195–96, 223–28.

[86]Treutlein, "Economic Regime," p. 296, quoting Pfefferkorn.

[87]Navarro García, *Sonora y Sinaloa,* p. 39.

[88]Zapata, "Relación de las misiones," p. 375–84; for more information on this document, *see* note 31 above.

[89]Pérez de Ribas, *Triunfos* 2: 26. Alegre, *Historia* 3: 10, describes diseases and epidemics in Sinaloa in 1641. Alegre describes how a *curandero,* or hechicero, of the Yaqui tried to cure a sick person but killed him instead. This tale might have been devised or exaggerated to discredit the hechiceros.

[90]Zapata, "Relación de las misiones," pp. 376, 382. Pfefferkorn, *Sonora,* p. 244, also describes the process of miscegenation in the mining towns, which usually resulted in losses to the mission population.

[91]It is necessary to investigate more thoroughly the nature of the labor force and the operational schedule of the mines to substantiate this hypothesis of seasonal workers. Did the mines function all year round, or were they short of workers during certain months and perhaps had to shut down temporarily? Did debt peonage develop in these mines, to tie the Indians down, or was labor scarcity too great and Indian mobility too high to permit widespread development of such an institution? These are some of the obvious questions. Unfortunately, I have not discovered much information or documents that relate directly to this matter.

[92]Bolton, *Rim,* pp. 126, 135.

[93]Bolton, *Rim,* p. 202. Father Kino's memoirs of his mission to the Pimería Alta have been made available in an English edition by Herbert E. Bolton: *Eusebio P. Kino, Historical Memoir of the Pimería Alta,* trans. by Herbert E. Bolton (Berkeley: University of California Press, 1948).

[94]Besides the summary histories of the California missions in Decorme, *Obra,* Alegre, *Historia,* and Bolton, *Rim,* the Jesuits who participated in this enterprise have left ample documentation and memoirs. The following are just a few of the more notable works, many of which are available in English translations: Eusebio E. Kino, *Kino Reports to Headquarters,* trans. and ed. by Ernest J. Burrus (Rome: Inst. Hist. S. J., 1954); Jakob Baegert, *Notícias de la penínsular americana de California* (Mexico: Antigua Lib. Robredo, 1942); Francisco Javier Clavijero, *Historia de la Antigua o Baja California* (Mexico: Impr. de J. R. Navarro, 1852); F. M. Pícolo, *Informe del estado de la nueva cristianidad de California, 1702,* trans. Ernest J. Burrus (Madrid: Ed. J. Porrús Turanzas, 1962); Juan María Salvatierra, *Selected Letters About Lower California,* trans. and annot. Ernest J. Burrus (Los Angeles: Dawson's Book Shop, 1971).

[95]Acosta, *Apuntes históricos,* p. 78; Bolton, *Rim,* pp. 446–47.

[96]Delfina E. López Sarrelange, "Misiones Jesuitas de Sonora y Sinaloa," *Estudios de Historia Novohispano,* no. 2 (1966): 195.

[97]Decorme, *Obra,* pp. 525–26.

[98]Decorme, *Obra,* p. 61; Pedro Tamarón y Romeral, *Demostración del vastísimo obispado de la Nueva Vizcaya, 1765, Durango, Sinaloa, Sonora, Arizona, Nuevo Mexico, Chihuahua y porciones de Texas, Coahuila y Zacatecas,* ed. by Vito Alessio Robles (Mexico: Antigua Lib. Rebredo de Porrúa, 1937), p. 265. Pedro de Rivera, "Informe al senor Virrey Marques de Casafuerte, sobre el estado de las misiones de la Compañía en las provincias de Sinaloa y Sonora, 1727," in *Documentos para la historia de México,* ser. 3, vol. 3, pp. 833–36; Acosta, *Apuntes históricos,* pp. 81–82.

[99]For discussions of these frontier Indian rebellions, *see* Jack D. Forbes, *Apache, Navaho and Spaniard* (Norman: University of Oklahoma Press, 1960) and Max L. Moorhead, *The Presidio. Bastion of the Spanish Borderlands* (Norman: University of Oklahoma Press, 1975). These authors have dubbed the series of frontier revolts in the late seventeenth century "The Great Northern Revolt," or "The Great Southwestern Revolt."

[100]Navarro García, *Sonora y Sinaloa,* p. 298; *see* pp. 292–308 for details of this rebellion which threatened to spread to the Yaqui territory.

[101]Navarro García, *Sonora y Sinaloa,* pp. 292–93. Some of the mission pueblos in Sonora had been under great pressure from Spanish vecinos since the beginning of the eighteenth century. In a long letter, one of the Sonora Jesuits charged vecinos of taking Indian land, forcing the Indians to work, and generally demoralizing them. "Representación del Padre Luis Pineli al Padre Pedro Matías Goñi sobre los graves daños que los indios padecen con los vecinos de su feligresia. Acontzi, 20 de octobre de 1709," copied on microfilm in the Instituto Nacional de Antropología e Historia. Fondo de Micropelicula. Sonora, Roll 21

(no pagination). Another document, dated 18 May 1716, illustrated the deteriorating condition of some of the mission pueblos in Sonora, reproduced in part in Lesley B. Simpson, *Studies in the Administration of the Indians of New Spain III: The Repartimiento System of Native Labor in New Spain and Guatemala,* Ibero-Americana, no. 13 (Berkeley: University of California Press, 1938), pp. 154–57, app. XI.

For an exhaustive but not always accurate listing of the Indian rebellions of the fifteenth to the seventeenth centuries in Nueva Vizcaya, *see* Galavíz de Capdevielle, *Rebeliones indígenas.* For the seventeenth century, she describes on pp. 37–38 a "rebelion de Zuaques, Ocoronis y Yaquis en la Villa de San Sebastián, 1696." This is the only reference anywhere to such a Yaqui rebellion. On closer examination, it becomes rather clear that Galavíz has hopelessly mixed up the dates of the Yaqui encounters with Captain Hurdaide at the beginning of the seventeenth century, not the end.

¹⁰² "Resumen de noticias correspondientes a Sinaloa, Rosario, Culiacán, Ostimuri y Sonora, y que comprenden desde 1734 hasta 1777," in *Documentos para la historia de México,* ser. 4, vol. 1, pp. 219–25.

Chapter 4

¹ The noted Spanish historian Luis Navarro García has written an account of the 1740 Yaqui rebellion: *La sublevación yaqui de 1740* (Sevilla: Escuela de Estudios Hispano-Americanos, 1966). He based his research on documents located in the Archivo de Indias in Sevilla, Spain. For a detailed description of these sources, *see* pp. 9–13 of his book. Also, Navarro García's work offers details on certain aspects of the rebellion which the present study summarizes.

Many of the documents Navarro García consulted in Sevilla are duplicated in the Pastells Collection of Rome, on microfilm at the Knights of Columbus Vatican Film Library St. Louis University, St. Louis, Missouri. The present analysis of the 1740 rebellion is based on the primary sources of the Pastells Collection. For more on the Pastells Collection, *see* Bibliography.

The most important document in Pastells is a compilation of copies of documents pertaining to the case, stretching over a period of some ten years. In June 1744, the Viceroy Conde de Fuenclara submitted to the Crown the final and definitive report on the rebellion. In addition to his own cover letter, he forwarded hundreds of pages of copied evidence from all parties involved in the conflict. Organized essentially in chronological order, these documents provide a detailed narrative of the uprising. Letter of Viceroy Conde de Fuenclara to His Majesty, 25 June 1744, Pastells 32: 323–712; hereafter cited as Fuenclara 1744. Unless otherwise noted, information contained in the present analysis comes from this source. Whenever necessary, specific documents in Fuenclara 1744 will be cited.

See also W. B. Stephens collection, Benson Latin American Collection, Univ. of Texas at Austin, Ms. no. 902.

² Fuenclara 1744 begins with an account of the 1735 clash between mineros and missionaries over the question of Indian laborers. Navarro García's study also

begins with this series of incidents, citing as his source a report Huidobro wrote in 1743. Huidobro did not just suddenly remember these incidents in 1743; he had actually filed routine reports on these events as they occurred. Then, in September 1740, during the rebellion, he wrote the viceroy railing against Jesuit abuses of Indians and disregard for secular authorities. In this letter he alluded to his earlier reports on the 1735 quarrels. *See* Huidobro to viceroy, Alamos, 4 September 1740, copied in Viceroy Duque de la Conquista report to Crown, Mexico, 9 October 1740, Pastells 29: 529–604.

³Quiroz to Huidobro, Los Cedros, 11 December 1735, in Fuenclara 1744, Pastells 32: 333–34.

According to Auditor de Guerra Marquéz de Altamira, whose lengthy report was included in Fuenclara 1744, the authorized quota of Indian workers was four percent of the adult male population from designated pueblos. Altamira also claimed that Lieutenant Governor Manuel de Mena rescinded Quiroz's order for calling up tapisques, in view of Quiroz's known hostility against the padres. *See* Auditor de Guerra Marquez de Altamira report, Mexico, 12 June 1743, in Fuenclara 1744, Pastells 32: 516–63.

⁴Fuenclara 1744, Pastells 32: 356–58. Lt. Gov. Mena, one of the fathers' few allies among local authorities, submitted the Jesuits' defense. There were several inconsistencies in his report. After claiming that Yaquis did not wish to travel the 60 leagues to work in Acevedo's mines, elsewhere he noted that Yaqui work teams often traveled as much as 400 leagues to look for work in mines. He also observed that one reason Yaquis sought mining work was because there were too many people for the available land in the mission. Unfortunately, he did not elaborate on the nature or causes of this situation, which would seem to be a most serious one. The issue of land would be brought up again, primarily by Yaquis and by missionaries, but not so much by Spaniards, who seemed more preoccupied in mid-eighteenth century over the shortage of laborers than scarcity of land.

Other sources confirm the long distances Yaquis often traveled to work in mines. Auditor Altamira stated that Yaquis were known to have traveled as much as 300 leagues to work in mines. *See* Altamira's report, 12 June 1743, in Fuenclara 1744, Pastells 32: 516–63.

⁵*See* the major Jesuit document on the 1740 rebellion entitled: "Hecho de la raíz, causas y progresos, hasta su conclusión de la rebelión de los Indios Hiaquis, Maios y Convezinos en la Gobernación de Sinaloa el año de 1740, siendo Gobernador Vitalicio Don Manuel Bernal de Huidobro," Pastells 18: 70–90. For more on this and other significant Jesuit documents on the 1740 rebellion, *see* note 22 below.

⁶The observations on how Nápoli and other fathers handled the food crisis and the sale of precious grains was made by Alcalde Acedo, whose report is contained in the report of Lic. Joseph Mexía de la Cerda y Vargas, 18 March 1744, Pastells 33:215–355.

⁷Juan Frías's testimony, taken by Huidobro, in Fuenclara 1744, Pastells 32: 391–92.

Fuenclara 1744 contains several summaries of the significant events from 1735 to the outbreak of rebellion in 1740. One of the best is Auditor Altamira's report, Pastells 32: 516–63 (already cited above). The auditor concurs that the rebellion began with the raids, in turn precipitated by the difficult times of recent years.

[8]The report on five casualties was contained in anti-Huidobro testimonies gathered by his rival and successor, Agustín de Vildósola. *See* Vecinos of Alamos, testimonies submitted by Vildósola to the viceroy, Alamos, 13 February 1743, Pastells 34: 385–438. In fleeing Ostimuri, the vecinos testified, they left behind five dead. When Huidobro and vecinos retreated from Cedros, rebels killed "a few" and took seventy women and children prisoners.

[9]Twelve vecinos, including Huidobro's brother Juan, testified that the governor dispatched men to the early trouble spots. These testimonies are included in Huidobro's appeal to the Crown for the return of his office, Mexico, 15 May 1741, Pastells 30: 175–243.

During his defense, Huidobro claimed that he was only following directions from higher-ups in employing *modos suaves* and waging a defensive, rather than offensive, war against the rebels. *See* Huidobro's response to the formal charges lodged against him, 6 February 1743, in Fuenclara 1744, Pastells 32: 473–95.

[10]Huidobro to Governor Belaunzarán of Nueva Vizcaya, to whom he appealed repeatedly for military aid, Baroyeca, 24 May 1740, in Viceroy Duque de la Conquista report to Crown, Mexico, 9 October 1740, Pastells 29: 529–604.

[11]Mendívil and Valenzuela were members of prominent Ostimuri families. As major property owners, they were naturally interested in an early conclusion to the violence and destruction. Another important Spanish family was the Lucenilla, headed by Gabriel and his brother Miguel, also a militia captain. They were the owners of the "gran hacienda de sacar plata por fuego y azoque de San Rafael de Los Cedros;" *see* Navarro García, *Sublevación*, p. 26. According to the Jesuits, the Quiroz and Lucenilla families were related. These families were among those vecinos who wrote the viceroy in 1736 denouncing Mena's actions at Pótam and thereby incurring the wrath of the Jesuits who were apparently behind the lieutenant governor.

The vecino and secular priest Pedro de Mendívil used the title *Bachiller*, denoting a university degree. The Jesuits used the similar title of *Licenciado*.

[12]Calixto himself testified that he rebelled because of the rumored deaths of Muni and Bernabé and that Father Nápoli had confirmed the rumors. *See* Fuenclara 1744, Pastells 32: 400. Mendívil also testified about the profound effects on Calixto of Muni's reported death and Father Nápoli's confirmation of the news. Mendívil to Huidobro, 20 January 1741, Pastells 30: 276–84.

[13]Accounts of these battles are in Fuenclara 1744, Pastells 32: 401–08. Vildósola's forces were composed of about thirty vecinos or militiamen and additional help from the Janos and Fronteras presidios of the northern frontier (exact number not specified). *See* Vecinos of Alamos, anti-Huidobro testimonies, gathered and submitted by Vildósola, Alamos, 13 February 1743, Pastells 34: 385–438. Vildósola expressed real fears that if not contained at the Sonoran border, the rebellion would infect the volatile Pimas Altos of

Sonora. His fears were well founded, for in 1751 the Pimas waged a rebellion similar in many respects to the 1740 Yaqui one. This rebellion will be discussed later in this chapter.

[14]Although it was Archbishop-Viceroy Vizarrón who had invited Muni and Bernabé to Mexico, it was his successor, Viceroy Duque de la Conquista, who actually received them, and considered their petition before sending them home to help with the pacification. The new viceroy's full name was: Pedro de Castro Figueroa y Salazar, Duque de la Conquista, Marquéz de Gracia Real.

According to Fuenclara 1744, in July 1740, upon hearing of the uprising and the false rumors concerning their deaths, Muni and Bernabé requested permission to return immediately to help pacify the rebels and that for this purpose and asked for and received appointments as captain-general and alférez, respectively; Fuenclara 1744, Pastells 32: 358.

[15]The orders regarding Huidobro's recall and the general amnesty were signed in October and November 1740 but did not reach the Yaqui until January 1741. The viceroy's mind was not always set so firmly against Huidobro. Up to October 1740 he balanced his judgment by noting Jesuit insensitivity to Yaqui needs along with Huidobro's incompetence. After Duque de la Conquista issued the amnesty in October, his mind began to vacillate. By November he had decided to remove Huidobro. In reports to the Crown in February and March 1741, he cited as causes of the rebellion only the *"mala conducta"* of Huidobro and his *"dependientes."* See Viceroy Duque de la Conquista to Crown, Mexico, 9 October 1740, Pastells 29: 529–604, *and* "Real Cédula de Don Pedro Castro Figueroa y Salazar, Duque de la Conquista, Marqués de García Real, etc. sobre tratamiento de los indios de Sinaloa y Sonora, 10 de octubre de 1740," in WBS/BLAC 902, pp. 1–2.

[17]Vildósola submitted several reports on his inspections of the Yaqui and Mayo missions in 1740 and 1741; *see* Vildósola to Viceroy Duque de la Conquista, Buenavista, 7 May 1740, Pastells 30: 364–75; and Sinaloa, 17 March 1741, Pastells 30: 149–71.

Vildósola began his gubernatorial career as a close Jesuit ally, assiduously collecting testimonies from many vecinos to bolster Jesuit charges against Huidobro. By helping to discredit Huidobro, he of course enhanced his own chances of becoming permanent governor. It is not clear whether Vildósola was actually appointed to conduct a formal *residencia,* or term-end review, of Huidobro, but he certainly acted as if he had been. For the anti-Huidobro testimonies he collected, *see:* Vecinos of Alamos, Alamos, 13 February 1743, Pastells 34: 385–438; Vecinos of Sinaloa, Sinaloa, 15 January 1743, Pastells 34: 629–35; Vecinos of Fuerte, Fuerte, 18 March 1743, Pastells 34: 636–41. In retaliation, Huidobro's partisans gathered testimonies critical of Vildósola as governor. One group charged that he freed some of the rebel chieftains whom Huidobro had imprisoned, consequently discouraging some Ostimuri vecinos from returning to the area. Some anti-Vildósola testimonies are included in Huidobro's appeal to the Crown, Mexico, 15 May 1741, Pastells 30: 175–243 and in Fuenclara 1744, dated 27 October 1741, Pastells 32: 439.

[18]The removal of Fathers González and Nápoli, the two most controversial missionaries, had been recommended for some time and by several senior advisors for the viceroy, including the *oidor,* or Audiencia judge, Antonio de Echevarri; *see* Echevarri to viceroy, Mexico, 24 September 1740, in Viceroy Duque de la Conquista to Crown, 9 October 1740, Pastells 29: 529–604.

[19]Vecinos of Alamos, anti-Huidobro testimonies, Alamos, 13 February 1743, Pastells 34: 385–438.

[20]Vildósola's reports to viceroy on the executions, Tórin, 1 August 1741, Pastells 30: 406. Fathers Arriola, García, and Anaya supported Vildósola's contention that the pacification was not complete until Muni and Bernabé were eliminated; *see* the fathers' enthusiastic report on Vildósola's actions in July and October 1741, Pastells 34: 442–45, and WBS/BLAC 902, pp. 59–74, 251–260.

Vildósola also maintained direct communication with Father Provincial Mateo Ansaldo himself. He echoed Jesuit sentiments in describing Muni as a "real Huidobrino" and a *"perillo de Huidobro."* *See* Vildósola to Ansaldo, 14 October 1742, in *Documentos para la historia de México,* ser. 4, vol. 1, p. 11. There are two other letters from Vildósola to Ansaldo, both dated 14 August 1742, in *Documentos para la historia de Mexico,* ser. 3, vol. 3, pp. 925–26, 929–30.

In one of the August letters, Vildósola made a very interesting observation which was not repeated in any other source. He accused Muni and supporters as *hechiceros,* or witches, because of the "peyote found in their pouches." This first and only reference to peyote that I have encountered in the colonial records suggests that certain aboriginal Yaqui customs had indeed survived well into the eighteenth century. Unfortunately, aside from suggesting a connection between witchcraft and peyote, Vildósola did not elaborate on its uses in any way or link it with the rebellion. Regrettably, the Yaquis' use of peyote cannot be pursued further in this study beyond this brief mention.

[21]A number of reports covered these events: Fuenclara 1744; Vecinos of Alamos, anti-Huidobro testimonies, Alamos, 13 February 1743, Pastells 34: 383–438; Vildósola to viceroy, Buenavista, 7 May 1741, Pastells 30: 364–72; Vildósola to viceroy, 11 July 1741, Pastells 30: 379–96; Vildósola to viceroy, Tórin, 1 August 1741, Pastells 30: 406.

[22]Ansaldo's untitled document is often referred to simply as "Representación del P. Mateo Ansaldo," also listed in the Pastells index as: "El P. Mateo Ansaldo Rector del Colegio de San Pedro y San Pablo de Méjico sobre la sublevación de los indios presente este escrito contra las injurias que el Huidobro pone en las autos que a los R. P. entregaron," 5 December 1743, Pastells 18: 91–104. Appended to this document is the Anonymous Report entitled: "Hecho de la Raiz, Causas y Progresos, hasta su conclusión de la rebelión de los Indios Hiaquis, Maios y convezinos en la Gobernación de Sinaloa el año de 1740, siendo Gobernador Vitalicio Don Manuel Bernal de Huidobro," Pastells 18: 72–90. Interestingly enough, Father Gerardo Decorme, noted twentieth century Jesuit historian, believes that the author of this anonymous report was none other than the controversial Father Diego González; *see* Decorme, *Obra,* p. 333. Unless otherwise noted, Jesuit views on the 1740 rebellion are from these two Jesuit documents. An

English translation of these documents is provided by John D. Meredith, "The Yaqui Rebellion of 1740: A Jesuit Account and Its Implications," *Ethnohistory* 22 (Summer 1975): 223–261.

According to Lic. Joseph Mexía de la Cerda y Vargas, who wrote an opinion favorable to the Jesuits, Ansaldo and fellow Jesuits demanded and obtained copies of important secular documents, including Muni and Bernabé's petition to the viceroy in 1739, and the reports and opinions of the Auditor de Guerra and the *fiscal* or Crown attorney, both senior advisors to the viceroy and both apparently more sympathetic to Huidobro and the Indians than to the Jesuits; Lic. Joseph Mexía de la Cerda y Vargas, Mexico, 18 March 1744, Pastells 33: 215–355.

In his sharply worded indictment, Ansaldo attacked not only Huidobro and dissident Yaquis, but those senior advisors with anti-Jesuit views. For example, he accused Auditor General de Guerra Pedro Malo Villavicencio of uncritically accepting Huidobro's unfounded accusations against the missionaries. For Malo's report to the viceroy, 2 August 1740, *see* Duque de la Conquista to Crown, 9 October 1740, Pastells 29; 529–604.

²³Lic. Joseph Mexía de la Cerda y Vargas, Mexico, 18 March 1744, Pastells 33: 236–37.

²⁴Perhaps the most specific discussion of Huidobro's personal conduct in office came from a group of anti-Huidobro vecinos, who maintained that he conducted a *comercio general* in the province and included a long list of abuses, graft, and other corrupt practices. It turned out that Jesuit Father Lucas Luis Álvarez of the Villa de Sinaloa had a hand in drafting this indictment, dated from Villa de Sinaloa, 5 December 1741. Tomás Huidobro produced twenty vecinos who repudiated every charge contained in the other statement. Nowhere else were these serious charges repeated or substantiated, nor did any of the high officials reviewing the case take up the charges seriously or conduct further investigations into them; these documents are included in Fuenclara 1744, Pastells 32: 465–69.

²⁵Fiscal's opinion, Mexico, 6 February 1743, Pastells 32: 495–515.

²⁶Alegre, *Historia* 4: 389–94.

²⁷Decorme, *Obra,* pp. 333–35.

²⁸Auditor de Guerra Marquez de Altamira, 12 June 1743, in Fuenclara 1744, Pastells 32: 516–63.

²⁹Quiroz's sentiments towards the Jesuits are quoted earlier in this chapter. Huidobro expressed his fears of Jesuit hegemony in several places; *see,* for example, Huidobro to Viceroy Duque de la Conquista, Alamos, 4 September 1740, Pastells 29: 583–90; Huidobro to Crown, Mexico, 15 May 1741, Pastells 30: 175–84.

³⁰Dunne, *Juan Antonio Balthasar,* pp. 64–65, describes Huidobro's disastrous relationship with the California Jesuits.

³¹Huidobro's formal reply to the Jesuit charges against him, 6 February 1743, in Fuenclara 1744, Pastells 32: 473–95. Among the local contemporaries who supported Huidobro's version of the causes of the rebellion was the vicar-general of Sinaloa, Pedro Gabriel de Aragón, whom Jesuits had identified as one of the governor's coconspirators. In an account he submitted to Bishop Tamarón y Romeral of Nueva Vizcaya many years later, in 1764, he emphasized Muni and Bernabé's complaints about coyotes and the fathers' highhanded, arbitrary

methods of discipline. He also argued that the "formal" cause of the rebellion was the famine, which forced many Yaquis to abandon their pueblos and steal food and cattle for survival. *See* Pedro Gabriel de Aragón to Bishop Pedro Tamarón y Romeral, 27 April 1764, in Tamarón y Romeral, *Demostración del vastísimo obispado de la Nueva Vizcaya, 1765. Durango, Sinaloa, Arizona, Nuevo México, Chihuahua y porciones de Texas, Coahuila y Zacatecas.* Intro., biblio., and annot. by Vito Alessio Robles. Biblioteca Historia Mexicana de Obras Inéditas, no. 7. (Mexico: Porrúa, 1937), pp. 417–19. Another contemporary account which basically followed Aragón's outline was the anonymous report titled: "Resumé of the news corresponding to Sinaloa, Rosario, Culiacán, Ostimuri and Sonora, which comprises from 1734 to 1777," in *Documentos para la historia de México,* ser. 4, vol. 1, pp. 219–35.

[32] As noted earlier in this chapter, even Huidobro's adversaries could account for only "a few" vecinos killed by rebels—five on one occasion; *see* Vecinos of Alamos, Alamos, 13 February 1743, Pastells 34: 385–438. Regarding property damages, one vecino, Sebastián Azcárraga, wrote his cousin Marcos Gaxiola, that the Lucenillas of Los Cedros alone lost 10,000 pesos. Azcárraga to Gaxiola, Sinaloa, 5 August 1740, Pastells 30: 462–65.

Several recent accounts of the rebellion have alleged without providing documentary evidence that 1000 or more (up to 3,000) Spaniards, or *gente de razón,* were killed by rebels, thereby perpetuating myths that arose around the rebellion shortly after its occurrence. The question is immediately raised whether there were that many Spaniards around the area to be killed. Not a single missionary was killed directly by rebels, and only about 100 vecinos—mainly women and children—were taken prisoners. Moreover, had there been that many victims, surely the outcry would have been louder and clearer in the hundreds of documents surrounding the case. Not a single senior official reviewing the case nor the official Jesuit commentaries even mentioned Spanish casualties in discussing consequences of the rebellion.

Accounting of Yaqui casualties has been equally elusive and unsubstantiable. Decorme, *Obra,* p. 339, with no supporting evidence, alleges that 2,000 to 3,000 Yaquis were killed in the battles of Tambor and Otancahui. Navarro García, *Sublevación,* p. 101, has determined that not only can this figure not be possible, but that the two battles themselves were mythical, that is, they never took place at all. Navarro García discusses some of the myths and legends that have arisen about the 1740 rebellion and the recent sources that have perpetuated these myths.

[33] See note 22 above. Also, interestingly, not only did the Jesuit Anonymous Report not discuss the content of the petition, but it mentioned Muni's and Bernabé's voyage to Mexico belatedly and incidentally, during the course of criticizing Archbishop-Viceroy Vizarrón's invitation to the dissident Indians.

[34] Muni's and Bernabé's petition to the viceroy, July 1739, in Fuenclara 1744, Pastells 32: 354–56.

[35] In gathering evidence against Huidobro, Muni, and Bernabé, Vildósola questioned several groups of witnesses over a period of time. In July 1741, he grilled a number of Yaqui principales or elders for damaging information. He

found one who testified that "Spaniards" had advised Muni to ask for secular priests and to pay tribute, but this Yaqui could not identify the Spaniard who allegedly gave such advice. Other Yaqui witnesses were unsure of what caused the rebellion, the raids, or Muni's instructions to rise up, and with whom Muni might have left such instructions; Vildósola to viceroy, Tórin, 13 July 1741, Pastells 30: 396–406. For another set of testimonies Vildósola gathered in the Yaqui, among Indians, coyotes, and Spaniards (67 individuals), *see* Vildósola to viceroy, Buenavista, 22 June 1741, in Fuenclara 1744, Pastells 32: 414–36.

[36]Auditor de Guerra Marquez de Altamira, 12 June 1743, in Fuenclara 1744, Pastells 32: 516–63; Fiscal's reports, Mexico, 6 February 1743, in Fuenclara 1744, Pastells 32: 495–515 (fiscal's name not given).

[37]Fuenclara's final decision on Huidobro is contained in his letter to the Crown, 25 June 1744, Pastells 33: 5–13; for his earlier decision, *see* letter to Crown, 9 November 1743, Pastells 33: 203.

[38]Fernando Sánchez Salvador, [Reports, n.d.], in *Documentos para la historia de México,* ser. 3, vol. 3, p. 639; Joseph Antonio Villaseñor y Sánchez, *Teatro americano; descripción general de los reynos y provincias de la Nueva España y sus jurisdicciones,* vol. 2 (Mexico: Impr. de la Vda. de D. Joseph Bernardo de Hogal, 1749), pp. 387–98.

[39]José Rafael Rodríguez Gallardo, [Reports, 1749–50], in Fernando Ocaranza, *Crónica y relaciones* 1: 141–73; also in *Documentos para la historia de México,* ser. 3, vol. 3, pp. 860–918; also in AGNM Historia 17 (no pagination). The citation here is from Ocaranza, pp. 170–71, which is the most readable copy. According to this report, there were fifty Jesuit missions, with three times as many branch pueblos or visitas, divided into six rectorados. Most were located in Sinaloa and Sonora, with a few in the Sierra Madre western slope and Baja California. Three visitor fathers supervised the activities of the missionaries in the field.

Villaseñor y Sánchez, *Teatro americano,* pp. 383, 388.

[40]For Balthasar's reports, *see* Dunne, *Juan Antonio Balthasar. See also* Vildósola's series of letters to Father Ansaldo in 1742, in *Documentos para la historia de México,* ser. 3, vol. 3, pp. 921–32; ser. 4, vol. 1, pp. 5–17. These letters are also summarized in Fernando Ocaranza, *Parva crónica de la Sierra Madre y las Pimerías* (Mexico: Ed. Stylo, 1942), pp. 149–52.

[41]For the history of the Pima Alta rebellion, *see* Russel C. Ewing, "The Pima Uprising of 1751: A Study of Spanish-Indian Relations on the Frontier of New Spain," in *Greater America,* pp. 259–80.

The irate and frustrated missionaries lumped Ortíz Parrilla with his predecessor, the hapless Huidobro, as "real monsters . . . as inept for their high positions as full of animosity towards the missionaries." They accused the governor and the vecinos of being totally responsible for the disastrous events of 1751 to 1752. *See* Ernest J. Burrus, *Misiones norteñas mexicanas de la Compañía de Jesús, 1751–57* (Mexico: Porrúa, 1963), p. 8.

[42]Rodríguez Gallardo, in Ocaranza, *Crónica y relaciones* 1:157, 166.

[43]Sánchez Salvador, in *Documentos para la historia de México,* ser. 3, vol. 3, pp. 638–51. Use of the term *mexicanización* may seem strange for the eighteenth

century, but it appeared several times in Sánchez Salvador's reports and obviously referred to the transformation of the advanced Mexico or Aztec civilization of central New Spain.

[44][Tomás] Ignacio Lizasaoín, "Informe sobre las provincias de Sonora y Nueva Vizcaya, rendido al Exmo. Sr. Virrey Marqués de Cruillas, s.f.," in *Documentos para la historia de México*, ser. 3, vol. 3, pp. 683–702. For some reason, Jesuits tended to take censuses by families. The ratio of approximately three individuals to one family has been noted in earlier and subsequent censuses. This small family size is puzzling, unless small children (under seven) were not counted or mobile adult males were missed in the count. Belém, with 265 families, was occupied mainly by Indians who were not Yaquis.

[45]Nentuig, *Rudo Ensayo*, p. 125.

[46]Juan Salgado to Juan Pineda, 27 October 1762, in *Documentos para la historia de México*, ser. 4, vol. 1, pp. 120–24; see also Father García's letter to Padre Visitador Lucas Atanasio Merino, 23 November 1760, in *Documentos para la historia de México*, ser. 4, vol. 1, pp. 104–20, on García's activities in organizing auxiliaries to defend Vícam and Tórin, two of the most frequently attacked pueblos.

[47]Och, *Missionary*, pp. 166–67.

[48]Lizasoaín, "Informe," in *Documentos para la historia de México*, ser. 3, vol. 3, pp. 689–90. He said that there were 50,000 persons in San Antonio in 1759. This must have been a misprint for 5,000, for there were hardly 50,000 persons in the entire northwest at this time, unless all mission Indians were included. *See* note 49 below for a partial breakdown of the population of the northwest.

[49]Tamarón y Romeral, *Demostración*, pp. 237–44, 247. The bishop gave a breakdown of the Spanish population of the northwest by towns, for a total of 12,057 persons, or 1,821 families. He also gave the population of some of the Indian pueblos, but cautioned against the reliability of the figures, for the most part supplied by parish priests. Most of all, he noted, it was difficult to count accurately the mobile Indians in the mining camps.

[50]Tamarón y Romeral, *Demostración*, pp. 246–47.

[51]Tamarón y Romeral, *Demostración*, p. 246. Inexplicably, while the Yaqui mission showed such a large population, the Mayo showed an incredibly low one of only 1,447 families, or 3,883 individuals; see Tamarón y Romeral, *Demostración*, pp. 240–41. The only explanation is that many Mayos left their pueblos, either to the mines or to the Yaqui mission, which were closer to the Sonoran mines.

[52]Nentuig, *Rudo Ensayo*, pp. 55–56. *See also* Och, *Missionary*, pp. 144–45, for his impressions of the conditions of the mining camps.

[53]Tamarón y Romeral, *Demostración*, p. 247.

[54]Navarro García has provided an exhaustive study of José de Gálvez in the northwest: Luis Navarro García, *Don José de Gálvez y la Comandancia General de las Provincias Internas del Norte de Nueva España* (Sevilla: Escuela de Estudios Hispano-Americanos, 1964). An earlier and more general study is Herbert I. Priestley, *José de Gálvez, Visitador-General of New Spain (1765–1771)* (Berkeley: University of California Press, 1916).

[55]Lorenzo Cancio to José de Gálvez, 31 October 1766, in *Documentos para la historia de México,* ser. 4, vol. 2, p. 176.

[56]Pineda circular, San Miguel de Horcasitas, in Alberto F. Pradeau, *La expulsión de los Jesuitas de las provincias de Sonora, Ostimuri y Sinaloa en 1767* (Mexico: Porrúa, 1959), pp. 159–60.

[57]Pradeau, *Expulsión,* p. 23, contains the names and missions of the ten missionaries; pp. 27–28 contain the orders from Viceroy Marqués de Croix to Pineda.

[58]Cancio to Pineda, 9 August 1767, in Pradeau, *Expulsión,* pp. 67–68.

[59]Cancio to Pineda, 1 October 1767, in Pradeau, *Expulsión,* p. 68.

[60]Cancio to Pineda, 9 August 1767, in Pradeau, *Expulsión,* pp. 67–68.

[61]Cancio to Pineda, 3 October 1767, in Pradeau, *Expulsión,* pp. 75–76.

[62]Cancio to Pineda, 20 December 1767, in Pradeau, *Expulsión,* pp. 80–81. *See also* pp. 169–72 for fragments of Father Francisco Ita's diary of the ordeal of expulsion from the missionaries' point of view.

[63]Cancio to Pineda, 27 May 1767, in *Documentos para la historia de México,* ser. 4, vol. 2, p. 196. Several of the letters reproduced in Pradeau, *Expulsión,* are also contained in *Documentos para la historia de México,* ser. 4, vol. 2, but some of the pages are not legible.

[64]Cancio letters, March–July 1768, in *Documentos para la historia de México,* ser. 4, vol. 2, pp. 251–78. At this point, 98 Guaymeno, 143 Pima Bajo, and 8 Sibupapa families had settled in Belém; *see* Cancio letter, 6 July 1768, in *Documentos para la historia de México,* ser. 4, vol. 2, p. 267.

[65]Cancio to Galindo y Quiñones, 28 January 1769, in *Documentos para la historia de México,* ser. 4, vol. 2, pp. 245–49.

[66]Cancio to Beleña, 4 March 1769, in *Documentos para la historia de México,* ser. 4, vol. 2, pp. 304–05.

[67]Cancio to Pineda, 20 October and 12 November 1768, in *Documentos para la historia de México,* ser. 4, vol. 2, pp. 281–85.

[68]Cancio letters, March–April 1769, in *Documentos para la historia de México,* ser. 4, vol. 2, pp. 207–15; Marques de Croix to Pineda, February–March 1769, in *Documentos para la historia de México,* ser. 4, vol. 2, pp. 12–15.

[69]Navarro García, *Gálvez,* pp. 174–75; Cancio letters, 29 May, 2 June, 6 June and 16 June 1769, in *Documentos para la historia de México,* ser. 4, vol. 2, pp. 36–46; Joaquín Valdés to Captain José Antonio Vildósola, 9 and 10 May 1770, in *Documentos para la historia de México,* ser. 4, vol. 2, pp. 343–48.

[70]Navarro García, *Gálvez,* p. 177.

[71]Gálvez to Elizondo and Pineda, 26 June, 2 July, 7 July and 16 July 1769, in *Documentos para la historia de México,* ser. 4, vol. 2, pp. 49–60.

[72]*See* Navarro García, *Gálvez,* pp. 178–85, for details of this campaign; *see also:* Elizondo's diary in *Documentos para la historia de México,* ser. 4, vol. 2, pp. 322–28; minutes of the junta of captains of the anti-Seri campaign, 9 November 1769, in *Documentos para la historia de México,* ser. 4, vol. 2, pp. 341–43. These minutes are also published as *Noticias breves de la expedición militar de Sonora y Sinaloa, su exito feliz y ventajoso estado en que por consecuencia de ella se han puesto*

ambas provincias, Mexico, 17 de junio de 1771 (Mexico: Vargas Rea, 1754). Apparently, the Sonora campaign had been a very trying experience for Gálvez, who was driven to temporary insanity.

[73]Marqués de Croix, "Instrucciones que deben observar mis comisionados para la asignación y repartimiento de tierras en los pueblos de indios de estas provincias y los de españoles que hubiere en el distrito de sus comisiones, y para la cuenta de tributarios que al mismo tiempo hacer en ellos. 1769," in *Documentos para la historia de México,* ser. 3, vol. 3, pp. 703–12. After the expulsion, the ex-Jesuit missions which were secularized were still referred to as missions.

Jesuit missions in Sonora, north of the Yaqui, were transferred to Franciscan missionary hands; *see* John L. Kessell, *Friars, Soldiers, and Reformers; Hispanic Arizona and the Sonora Mission Frontier, 1767–1856* (Tucson: University of Arizona Press, 1976).

[74]Marqués de Croix, "Segunda instrucción práctica que han de observar los comisionados para el repartimiento de tierras en los pueblos de los cuatro ríos de Sinaloa, Fuerte, Mayo y Yaqui, 1771," reissued on 12 August 1778, in *Documentos para la historia de México,* ser. 3, vol. 3, pp. 713–17.

[75]Navarro García, *Gálvez,* p. 252.

[76]Navarro García, *Gálvez,* p. 254.

[77]Sastre to viceroy, "Sobre los sistemas administrativos de las misiones, y proyecto de reformas en el gobierno temporal y espiritual de las minas," 16 December 1772; and Viceroy to Commander General Jacobo Ugarte y Loyola, Mexico, 26 August 1786, on microfilm in Instituto Nacional de Antropoligía e Historia. Fondo de Micropelícula. Sonora, roll 23.

[78]Bernardo de Gálvez, *Instructions for Governing the Interior Provinces of New Spain, 1786,* trans. and ed. by Donald E. Worcester. Quivira Society Pub., vol. 12 (Berkeley: Quivira Society, 1951), p. 58. This collection of documents reproduces the original Spanish with facing English translations. The original Spanish of this citation is on p. 119.

[79]Antonio de los Reyes, "Relación de todas las misiones establecidas en la diócesis de Sonora (Sonora, September 15, 1784)," in Hermes Tovar Pinzón, ed., *Lecturas de historia social y económica, Colombia y America: fuentes para el estudio de las actividades socio-económicas de la Compañía de Jesús y otras misiones religiosas* (Bogatá: Univ. Nac. de Colombia, 1971), pp. 79–86. This is perhaps the most detailed report on conditions in the ex-Jesuit missions in the late eighteenth century. A biography of Bishop de los Reyes has appeared, apparently written by one of his descendents: Albert Stagg, *The First Bishop of Sonora, Antonio de los Reyes, O.F.M.* (Tucson: University of Arizona Press, 1976).

[80]Valdés to Grimarest, in Ocaranza, *Crónica* 2: 282–83; Jacinto Álvarez, "Subdelegado de la Provincia de San Ildefonso de Ostimuri," Report c. 1804, in Ocaranza, *Crónica* 2: 297.

[81]Reyes, "Relación," in Pinzón, *Lecturas,* pp. 81–82.

[82]Fray Antonio de los Reyes, "Noticia del estado actual de las misiones que en la gobernación de Sonora administran los padres del Colegio de Propaganda Fide de la Santa Cruz de Querétaro," 20 April 1772, in *Documentos para la historia de*

México, ser. 3, vol. 3. pp. 724–65; also copied on microfilm in Instituto Nacional de Antropología e Historia, Fondo de Micropelícula. Sonora, roll 23.

The energetic new bishop of Sonora painted a gloomy, depressing picture of the sad fate that had befallen the missions of Sonora, Ostimuri, and Sinaloa when he visited that area in 1784. Most of the Indian pueblos, including those between the Yaqui and Mayo rivers, had been abandoned by their original Indian inhabitants and taken over completely by "vagrants, thieves and bums." Even the Mayo pueblos were not doing well, for "Spaniards, mulattoes and other mixed-bloods" had invaded them, in some cases dislodging the Mayos, forcing them consequently to "live lazily, dispersed and vagrant in the reales de minas, haciendas and ranches of the Spaniards, robbing and increasing the disorder of these unfortunate pueblos and provinces"; *see* his relación in Pinzón, *Lecturas,* pp. 56–114.

[83]Reyes, "Relación," in Pinzón, *Lecturas,* pp. 79–86.

[84]Reyes, "Relación," in Pinzón, *Lecturas,* p. 81.

[85]Reyes, "Relación," in Pinzón, *Lecturas,* p. 81; Marques de Croix, "Instrucciones," in *Documentos para la historia de México,* ser. 3, vol. 3, pp. 703–12.

[86]Felipe de Jesús Álvarez to Marín, Pótam, 1 June 1784, and Marín to Commander General Pedro de Nava, 13 January 1795, both on microfilm in the Instituto Nacional de Antropología e Historia. Fondo de Micropelícula. Sonora, roll 14.

[87]Reyes, "Relación," in Pinzón, *Lecturas,* p. 80; Ocaranza, *Crónica* 2: 81–82.

[88]Reyes, "Relación," in Pinzón, *Lecturas,* p. 81; Ocaranza, *Crónica* 2: 298.

[89]Joaquín Valdés, Report to Intendent and Governor Enrique de Grimarest, 1790, in Ocaranza, *Crónica* 2: 282–83.

[90]Joaquín Valdés, Report to Grimarest, in Ocaranza, *Crónica* 2: 285–86; Ocaranza, *Crónica* 2: 297–98.

Bibliography

Archives (unpublished material)

Archivo General de la Nación de México. Mexico City (AGNM).
Many *ramos,* or departments, were scrutinized, but only the following yielded a few important documents on Jesuits, Yaquis, and the northwest during the colonial period: Provincias Internas, JHS (Jesuits), and Historia.

Bancroft Library. University of California. Berkeley, California.
This archive has collected many of the Jesuit *cartas anuas,* or annual reports, from the Mexican missions. These reports, most of them copies of the original, are bound in two collections: "Memorias para la historia de Sonora," and "Documentos para la historia de Sinaloa," 2 vols.

Instituto Nacional de Antropología e Historia. Fondo de Micropelícula. Mexico City.

The Institute has undertaken a vast project to collect, centralize, and preserve on microfilm the state archives of Mexico, as well as other special historical archives. The Sonora collection has 23 rolls of over 1000 frames each (frames not numbered).

Knights of Columbus Vatican Film Library. Pius XII Memorial Library. St. Louis University, St. Louis, Missouri. Pastells Collection.

At the end of the nineteenth century, Father Pablo Pastells y Vila directed a group of diligent Jesuit scribes to copy by hand all documents dealing with Jesuit activities overseas contained in the Archivo de Indias in Seville, Spain. The collection is in Rome. St. Louis University has microfilmed the entire collection. For a history and detailed description of the Pastells Collection, *see:* F. Mateos, S. J., "La Colección Pastells de documentos sobre América y Filipinas." *Revista de Indias,* no. 27 (January–March, 1947), pp. 7–52. This collection contains all the important documents dealing with the 1740 Yaqui rebellion.

Collections of Documents, Books, Articles and Miscellaneous Works (published materials)

Acosta, Roberto. *Apuntes históricos sonorenses. La conquista temporal y espiritual del Yaqui y el Mayo.* Mexico: Impr. Aldina, 1949.

Alegre, Francisco Javier. *Historia de la provincia de la Compañía de Jesús de Nueva España.* 4 vols. New edition by Ernest J. Burrus and Felix Zubillaga. Rome: Inst. Hist. S. J., 1956.

Written in the late eighteenth century. A 1940 Mexican edition was entitled: *Memorias para la historia de la provincia que tuvo la Compañía de Jesús en Nueva España.*

Alessio Robles, Vito. "Las condiciones sociales en el norte de la Nueva España." *Academia Mexicana de la Historia. Memorias* 4 (April–June 1945): 139–157.

_____. *Francisco de Urdiñola y el norte de la Nueva España.* Mexico: Impr. Mundial, 1931.

Almada, Francisco R. *Diccionario de historia, geografía y biografía sonorenses.* Chihuahua: n.p., 1952.

One of the most important and useful reference works; an invaluable compilation of information.

Arlegui, José. *Crónica de la Provincia de N.S.P.S. Francisco de Zacatecas.* Mexico: n.p., 1737.

Arricívita, Juan Domingo. *Crónica seráfica y apostólica de propaganda fide de la Santa Cruz de Querétaro de Nueva España.* Segunda parte. Mexico: n.p., 1792.

Astraín, Antonio. *Historia de la Compañía de Jesús en la asistencia de España.* 5 vols. Madrid: n.p., 1902.

Baegert, Jakob. *Noticias de la penínsular americana de California.* Mexico: Antigua Lib. Robredo, 1942.
First published in German in 1772.

_____. *Observations in Lower California.* Translated from the original German with notes and introduction by M. M. Brandenburg and Carl L. Baumann. Berkeley: University of California Press, 1952.

Bakewell, Peter John. *Silver Mining and Society in Colonial Mexico: Zacatecas, 1546–1700.* Cambridge: Cambridge University Press, 1971.

Bancroft, Hubert Howe. *Works.* 39 vols. *The Native Races. Wild Tribes.* Vol 1. *History of the North American States, 1531–1800.* Vol. 15. San Francisco: A. L. Bancroft, 1882–1890.

Bandelier, Adolph F. *The Gilded Man.* New York: Appleton, 1893.

Bannon, John Francis. "Black Robe Frontiersman: Pedro Méndez, S.J." *Hispanic American Historical Review* 27 (February 1948): 61–86.

_____. *Indian Labor in the Spanish Indies. Was There Another Solution?* Problems in Latin American Civilization Series. Boston: D. C. Heath & Co., 1966.

_____. *The Mission Frontier in Sonora, 1620–1687.* U.S. Catholic Historical Society Monograph Series, no. 26. New York: U. S. Catholic Historical Society, 1955.

Basauri, Carlos. *La población indígena de México. Etnografía.* Mexico: Sría. de Educ. Púb., 1940.

Bayle, Constantino. *Historia de los descubrimientos y colonización de los padres de la Compañía de Jesús en la Baja California.* Madrid: V. Suárez, 1933.

Beals, Ralph L. *The Aboriginal Culture of the Cáhita, Indians.* Ibero-Americana, no. 19. Berkeley: University of California Press, 1943.

_____. *The Comparative Ethnology of Northern Mexico Before 1750.* Ibero-Americana, no. 2. Berkeley: University of California Press, 1932.

_____. *The Contemporary Culture of the Cáhita Indians.* Smithsonian Institution. Bureau of American Ethnology Bulletin. Washington, D.C.: 1945.

Bennett, Wendell C. and Zingg, Robert M. *The Tarahumara: An Indian Tribe of Northern Mexico.* Chicago: University of Chicago Press, 1935.

Benson Latin American Collection. University of Texas at Austin, Austin, Texas. W. B. Stephens collection (WBS/BLAC).
Consisting of rare books and manuscripts dealing primarily with the early history of Texas, New Mexico, Arizona and California, the Stephens collection includes many original Jesuit documents of northern New Spain.

Bolton, Herbert Eugene. *Coronado. Knight of Pueblos and Plains.* Albuquerque: University of New Mexico Press, 1949.

_____. "The Mission as a Frontier Institution in the Spanish-American Colonies." *American Historical Review* 23 (October 1917): 42–61.

_____. *The Padre on Horseback.* Chicago: Loyola University Press, 1963.

_____. *Rim of Christendom. A Biography of Eusebio Francisco Kino, Pacific Coast Pioneer.* New York: Macmillan Co., 1936.

Brading, David. *Miners and Merchants in Bourbon Mexico, 1763–1810.* Cambridge: Cambridge University Press, 1971.

Buelna, Eustaquio. *Arte de la lengua Cáhita, por un padre de la Cía. de Jesús.* Mexico: Impr. de Gobierno Federal, 1891.

Burrus, Ernest J., ed. *Misiones norteñas mexicanas de la Compañía de Jesús, 1751–1757.* Biblioteca Historia Mexicana de Obras Inéditas, no. 25. Mexico: Porrúa, 1963.

_____. *La obra cartográfica de la Provincia Mexicana de la Compañía de Jesús.* 2 vols. Madrid: Ed. José Porrúa Turanzas, 1967.
Listing and reproduction of Jesuit maps.

Cabeza de Vaca, Alvar Núñez. *The Journey of Alvar Núñez Cabeza de Vaca and His Companions from Florida to the Pacific, 1528–1536.* Translated by Fanny Bandelier. New York: Allerton Book Co., 1922.

_____. *Relation of Alvar Núñez Cabeza de Vaca.* Translated by Buckingham Smith. New York: n.p., 1871.

Castañeda, Carlos. *The Teaching of Don Juan: A Yaqui Way of Knowledge.* Berkeley: University of California Press, 1968.

_____. *A Separate Reality: Further Conversations with Don Juan.* New York: Simon and Schuster, 1971.

_____. *Journey to Ixtlán: The Lessons of Don Juan.* New York: Simon and Schuster, 1972.

Castillo, Ricardo M. "Sobre el establecimiento de la Comandancia General en las Provincias Internas del Norte, 1771." *Archivo General de la Nación. Boletín* 12 (1941): 75–82.

Clavijero, Francisco Javier. *Historia de la Antigua o Baja California.* Mexico: Impr. de J. R. Navarro, 1852.

————. *History of Lower California.* Riverside, California: Manessier Pub. Co., 1971, c. 1937.

Cleaver, Harry M. "The Contradictions of the Green Revolution." *Monthly Review* 24 (1972): 80–111.

Colección de documentos inéditas relativo al descubrimiento, conquista y colonización de las posesiones españoles en América y Oceanía, sacados en su mayor partes, del Real Archivo de Indias, bajo la dirección de los Sres. D. Joaquín F. Pacheco y D. Fco. de Cárdenas. 42 vols. Madrid: n.p., 1864–1884.
This collection is also known as the *Documentos inéditas de Indias.* It has an index by name and by date.

Dávila, Tomás. *Sonora histórica y descriptiva.* Reseña histórica desde la llegada de los españoles y una descripción de sus terrenos de agricultura y pasturaje, su minería y cría de ganada, sus bosques, ríos, montañas y valles, sus ciudades, pueblos. Nogales, Arizona: Tip. de R. Bernal, 1894.

Dobie, James Frank. *Apache Gold and Yaqui Silver.* London: Hammond, Hammond & Co., 1956.

Decorme, Gerardo. *La obra de los Jesuitas mexicanos durante la época colonial, 1572–1767.* Vol. 2. *Las misiones.* Mexico: Antigua Lib. Robredo de J. Porrúa e Hijos, 1941.

Documentos para la historia de México. 20 vols. in 4 series. Mexico: Manuel Orozco y Berra, 1907.
This collection contains many important documents of the northwest, including letters written by colonial officials. It has an index prepared by Genaro García.

Dunbier, Roger. *The Sonoran Desert. Its Geography, Economy and People.* Tucson: University of Arizona Press, 1968.

Dunne, Peter M. *Andrés Pérez de Ribas. Pioneer Black Robe of the West Coast, Administrator, Historian.* New York: U.S. Catholic Historical Society, 1951.

————. *Black Robes in Lower California.* Berkeley: University of California Press, 1952.

————. *Early Jesuit Missions in Tarahumara.* Berkeley: University of California Press, 1948.

Dunne, Peter M. *(continued)*

————. [trans. and ed.]. *Juan Antonio de Balthasar, Padre Visitador to the Sonoran Frontier, 1744–1745.* Tucson: Arizona Pioneer Historical Society, 1957. Translation of two reports by Father Balthasar.

————. *Pioneer Black Robes on the West Coast.* Berkeley: University of California Press, 1940.

————. *Pioneer Jesuits in Northern Mexico.* Berkeley: University of California Press, 1944.

Fábila, Alfonso. *Los indios Yaquis de Sonora.* Mexico: Sría de Educ. Púb., 1945.

Flores Guerrero, Raúl. "El imperialismo Jesuita en la Nueva España." *Historia Mexicana* 4 (October–December 1954): 159–73.

Forbes, Jack D. *Apache, Navaho and Spaniards.* Norman: University of Oklahoma Press, 1960.

Galavíz de Capdevielle, María Elena. *Rebeliones indígenas en el norte del Reino de la Nueva España, XVI–XVII.* Mexico: Ed. Campesina, 1967.

Gálvez, Bernardo de. *Instructions for Governing the Interior Provinces of New Spain, 1786.* Translated and edited by Donald L. Worcester. Quivira Society Pub., vol. 12. Berkeley: Quivira Society, 1951.
Contains some documents in the original Spanish with facing English translation.

Gamboa, Francisco Javier de. *Comentarios de la Ordenanzas de Minas.* Madrid: Oficina de Joaquín Ibarra, 1761.
A very useful source for the study of mining in colonial Mexico. Chapter 28 contains a list of mines in operation at time of writing.

Gibson, Charles. *The Aztecs Under Spanish Rule.* Stanford: Stanford University Press, 1964.

Giddings, Ruth Warner. *Yaqui Myths and Legends.* Tucson: University of Arizona Press, 1959.

Greater America. Essays in Honor of Herbert Eugene Bolton. Berkeley: University of California Press, 1945.

Hackett, Charles Wilson, ed. *Historical Documents Relating to New Mexico, Nueva Vizcaya and Approaches Thereto, to 1773.* Collected by A. Bandelier and Fanny R. Bandelier. 3 vols. Washington, D.C.: Carnegie Institute, 1923.
The first two volumes contain the original Spanish with English translations. The third does not include the Spanish.

Hammond, George P. *The Adventure of Don Francisco Vásquez de Coronado.* Albuquerque: University of New Mexico Press, 1938.

Handbook of Middle American Indians. Edited by Robert Wauchope. *Ethnology.* Vol. 8. Pt. 2. Edited by Evon Z. Vogt. Austin: University of Texas Press, 1969.

Hernández, Fortunato. *Las razas indígenas de Sonora y las guerras del Yaqui.* Mexico: Casa Edit. J. de Elizalde, 1902.

Herrera Carrillo, Pablo. "Sinaloa a mediados del siglo XVII." *Congreso Mexicano de Historia. Memorias y Revistas* 1 (1960): 145–174.

Hewitt de Alcántara, Cynthia. *Modernizing Mexican Agriculture: Socioeconomic Implications of Technological Change 1940–1970.* Geneva: United Nations Research Institute for Social Development, 1976.

Hinton, Thomas B. *A Survey of Indian Assimilation in Eastern Sonora.* Tucson: University of Arizona Press, 1959.

Hodge, Frederick W., ed. *Handbook of American Indians North of Mexico.* 2 vols. Bureau of American Ethnology Bulletin, no. 30. Washington, D.C., 1907–1910.

Huerta Preciado, Maria Teresa. *Rebeliones indígenas en el noroeste de México en la época colonial.* Mexico: Instituto Nacional de Antropología e Historia, 1966.

Humboldt, Alexandro de. *Ensayo político sobre Nueva España.* Notas y arreglo por V. Alessio Robles. Mexico: Ed. Robredo, 1941.

Icazbalceta, Joaquín García. *Colección de documentos para la historia de México.* 2 vols. Mexico: Antigua Librería, 1866.

Jacobsen, Jerome V. *Educational Foundations of the Jesuits in 16th Century New Spain.* Berkeley: University of California Press, 1938.

———. "Pedro Sánchez, Founder of the Jesuits in New Spain." *Mid-America* 22 (July 1940): 157–190.

Johnson, Jean B. *El idioma Yaqui.* Mexico: Instituto Nacional de Antropología e Historia, 1962.

Kessell, John L. *Friars, Soldiers and Reformers; Hispanic Arizona and the Sonoran Mission Frontier, 1767–1856.* Tucson: University of Arizona Press, 1976.

———. *Mission of Sorrow: Jesuit Guevavi and the Pimas, 1691–1767.* Tucson: University of Arizona Press, 1970.

Kino, Eusebio Francisco. *Historical Memoirs of the Pimería Alta.* Translation of the *Favores Celestiales,* by Herbert E. Bolton. Berkeley: University of California Press, 1948.

———. *Kino Reports to Headquarters.* Edited by Ernest J. Burrus. Rome: Inst. Hist. S.J., 1954.
Contains Kino's correspondence with Mexico and Rome.

Kino, Eusebio Franciso *(continued)*
_____. *Las misiones de Sonora y Arizona.* Mexico: Ed. Cultura, 1913–22. Composed of the *Favores Celestiales* and *Relación diaria de la entrada del noroeste.*

Kirchhoff, Paul. "Gatherers and Farmers in the Greater Southwest," *American Anthropologist,* n.s. 56 (August 1954): 529–550.

Kroeber, A. L. *Cultural and Natural Areas of Native North America.* Berkeley: University of California Press, 1939.

_____. *Uto-Aztecan Languages of Mexico.* Ibero-Americana, no. 8. Berkeley: University of California Press, 1934.

Kurath, William and Spicer, Edward H. *A Brief Introduction to Yaqui. A Native Language of Sonora.* University of Arizona Bulletin, vol. 18, no. 1, Social Science Bulletin, no. 15 (January 1947).

López-Portillo y Weber, José. *La rebelión de Nueva Galicia.* Instituto Panamericano de Geografía e Historia Pub., no. 37. Mexico: IPGH, 1939.

Mange, Juan Mateo. *Luz de tierra incognita en la América septentrional y diario de las exploraciones en Sonora.* Mexico: Archivo General de la Nación de México, 1926.

_____. *Luz de Tierra Incognita, Unknown Arizona and Sonora, 1693–1701.* Translated and adapted by Harry J. Karns. Tucson: Arizona Silhouettes, 1954.

Mecham, J. Lloyd. *Francisco de Ibarra and Nueva Vizcaya.* Durham: Duke University Press, 1927.

Mendizábal, Miguel Othón de. "La evolución del noroeste de México." In *Obras Completas,* vol. 3, pp. 7–86. Mexico: n.p., 1946.

Meredith, John D. "The Yaqui Rebellion of 1740: A Jesuit Account and Its Implications." *Ethnohistory* 22 (Summer 1975): 223–261.

Moorhead, Max. *The Apache Frontier. Jacobo Ugarte and Spanish Indian Relations in Northern New Spain, 1769–1791.* Norman: University of Oklahoma Press, 1968.

_____. *The Presidio. Bastion of the Spanish Borderland.* Norman: University of Oklahoma Press, 1975.

Mota Padilla, Matías de la. *Historia de la conquista del reino de la Nueva Galicia,* escrita por el Lic. D. Matías de la Mota Padilla en 1742. Guadalajara: n.p., 1920.

Mota y Escobar, Alonso de la. *Descripción geográfica de los reinos de Nueva Galicia, Nueva Vizcaya y Nuevo León.* Mexico: Robredo, 1940. Written c. 1600.

Navarro García, Luis. *Don José de Gálvez y la Comandancia General de las Provincias Internas del Norte de Nueva España.* Sevilla: Escuela de Estudios Hispano-Americanos, 1964.

————. *La sociedad rural de México en el siglo XVIII.* Sevilla: Escuela de Estudios Hispano-Americanos, 1963.

————. *Sonora y Sinaloa en el siglo XVII.* Sevilla: Escuela de Estudios Hispano-Americanos, 1967.

————. *La sublevación Yaqui de 1740.* Sevilla: Escuela de Estudios Hispano-Americanos, 1966.

[Nentuig, Juan]. *Rudo Ensayo, By An Unknown Jesuit Padre. 1763.* Tucson: Arizona Silhouettes, 1951.
  This is a reproduction of an earlier publication with the same title, translated by Eusebio Guiteras, Records of the American Catholic Historical Society of Philadelphia, vol. 5, no. 2 (1894). A slightly different version of this same document appears in AGNM Historia 16: 8–137; AGNM Historia 383 (no pagination); and *Documentos para la historia de México*, ser. 3, vol. 1: 489–637, under the title: "Descripción geográfica natural y curiosa de la Provincia de Sonora, por un Amigo del Servicio de Dios; y del Rey Nuestro Señor. Año de 1764."

Noticia breve de la expedición militar de Sonora y Sinaloa, su escito feliz y ventajoso estado en que por consecuencia de ella se han puesto ambas provincias. Mexico 17 de junio de 1771. Mexico: Vargas Rea, 1954.
  Sometimes cited as "Breve historia de la expedición militar de Sonora y Sinaloa, 1771."

Obregón, Balthasar de. *Historia de la descubrimientos antiguos y modernos de la Nueva España. Año de 1584.* Mexico: Dpto. Ed. de la Sría. de Educ. Púb., 1924.

————. *Obregón's History of 16th Century Explorations in Western America, entitled Chronicle, Commentary or Relation of the Ancient and Modern Discoveries in New Spain and New Mexico, Mexico 1584.* Translated, edited and annotated by George P. Hammond. Los Angeles: Wetzel Pub. Co., 1928.

Ocaranza, Fernando. *Crónica de las provincias internas de la Nueva España.* Mexico: Ed. Polis, 1939.

————. *Crónica y relaciones del occidente de México.* 2 vols. Mexico: Antigua Lib. Robredo de José Porrúa e Hijos, 1937.

————. *Parva Crónica de la Sierra Madre y las Pimerías.* Mexico: Ed. Stylo, 1942.

Och, Joseph. *Missionary in Sonora, 1755–1767.* Translated by Theodore Treutlein. San Francisco: California Historical Society, 1965.

Orozco y Berra, Manuel. *Historia de la dominación española en México.* Vol. 3. Biblioteca Historia Mexicana de Obras Inéditas, no. 10. Mexico: José Porrúa, 1938.

————. *Geografía de las lenguas y cartas etnográficas de México.* Mexico: Impr. de J. M. Andrade y F. Escalante, 1864.

Ortega, José. *Historia del Nayarit, Sonora y Sinaloa y Ambas Californias con el título de "Apostólicos afanes de la Compañía de Jesús en la América Septentrional."* 3 vols. New edition with prologue by Miguel de Olaguibel. Mexico: Tip. de E. Abadiano, 1887.

Actually, only volume 1, entitled "Apostólicos afranes," was written by Ortega; volumes 2 and 3 were written by Father Juan Antonio Balthasar about the Jesuit fathers Kino, Keller, Consag, and Sedelmayr.

Pérez de Ribas, Andrés. *Historia de los triunfos de N.S. Fe entre gentes las más bárbaras y fieras del Nuevo Orbe.* 3 vols. Mexico: Ed. Layac, 1944. Written in 1645.

————. *Crónica y historia relativa de la provincia de la Compañía de Jesús de México en Nueva España.* Mexico: Impr. del Sagrada Corazón de Jesús, 1896.

Pfefferkorn, Ignaz. *Sonora. A Description of the Province.* Translated and annotated by Theodore Treutlein. Albuquerque: University of New Mexico Press, 1949.

Written in German and first published in Germany in 1794–95.

Phelan, John. "Authority and Flexibility in the Spanish Imperial Bureaucracy." *Administrative Science Quarterly* 5 (1940), 47–65.

Pícolo, Francisco María. "Descubrimiento por tierra de la contra costa y otros pasajes de tierra." In *Tres Documentos sobre el descubrimiento y exploración de Baja California.* Edited by Roberto Ramos. Mexico: Ed. Jus, 1958.

————. *Informe del estado de la nueva cristianidad de California, 1702.* Edited by Ernest J. Burrus. Mexico: Ed. J. Porrúa Turanzas, 1962.

————. *Informe of the New Province of California, 1702.* Translated by George Hammond. Los Angeles: Dawson Book Shop, 1967.

Pimentel, Francisco. *Cuadro descriptivo y comparativo de las lenguas indígenas de México.* 3 vols. Mexico: Tip. de I. Epstein, 1874–1875.

Pinzón, Hermes Tovar, ed. *Lecturas de historia social y económica, Colombia y América. Fuentes para el estudio de las actividades socioeconómicas de la Compañía de Jesús y otras misiones religiosas.* Bogatá: Univ. Nac. de Colombia, Fac. de Ciencias Humanas, 1971.

Polzer, Charles W. *Rules and Precepts of the Jesuit Missions of Northwestern New Spain.* Tucson: University of Arizona Press, 1976.

Pradeau, Alberto Francisco. "Descripción de Sonora del Padre Nentuig." *Archivo General de la Nación. Boletín* 26 (1955): 239–253.

_____. *La expulsión de los Jesuitas de las provincias de Sonora, Ostimuri y Sinaloa en 1767.* Biblioteca Historia Mexicana de Obras Inéditas, no. 24. Mexico: Porrúa, 1959.

Priestley, Herbert I. *José de Gálvez, Visitador-General of New Spain, (1765–1771).* Berkeley: University of California Press, 1916.

Reyes, Antonio de los. *Copia del manifesto Estado de la Provincias de Sonora. 20 de abril de 1772.* Mexico: Biblioteca Aportación Histórica Ed. Vargas Rea, 1945.

Rivera, Pedro de. *Diario y derrotero de lo caminado, visto y observado en la visita que hizo a los presidios del Nueva España septentrional.* Introduction and notes by Vito Alessio Robles. Archivo Histórico Militar Mexicano, no. 2. Mexico: Sría. de la Defensa Nacional. Dirección de Archivo Militar, 1946.
First published in 1736.

Sahlins, Marshall. *Stone Age Economics.* Chicago: Aldine Atherton, 1972.

Salvatierra, Juan María. *Selected Letters About Lower California.* Translated and annotated by Ernest J. Burrus. Los Angeles: Dawson's Book Shop, 1971.

Sánchez-Barba, Mario Hernández. *La última expansión española en América.* Madrid: Instituto de Estudios Políticos, 1957.

Saravia, Atanasio. *Apuntes para la historia de la Nueva Vizcaya. La conquista.* Vol. 1. *La ciudad de Durango.* Vol. 2. *Las sublevaciones.* Vol. 3. Mexico: Manuel Porrúa, n.d.

Sarrelange, Delfina E. López. "Misiones Jesuitas de Sonora y Sinaloa." *Estudios de Historia Novohispano,* no. 2 (1966): 149–201.

Sauer, Carl O. *The Aboriginal Population of Northwest Mexico.* Ibero-Americana, no. 10. Berkeley: University of California Press, 1935.

_____. *The Distribution of Aboriginal Tribes and Languages in Northwestern Mexico.* Ibero-Americana, no. 5. Berkeley: University of California Press, 1934.

_____. *The Road to Cíbola.* Ibero-Americana, no. 3. Berkeley: University of California Press, 1932.

_____ and Brand, Donald. *Aztatlán. Prehistoric Mexican Frontier on the Pacific Coast.* Ibero-Americana, no. 1. Berkeley: University of California Press, 1932.

Shiels, William E. *Gonzalo de Tapia (1561–1584)*. U. S. Catholic Historical Society Monograph Series, no. 14. New York: U. S. Catholic Historical Society, 1934.

Simpson, Lesley B. *Studies in the Administration of the Indians of New Spain. III. The Repartimiento System of Native Labor in New Spain and Guatemala*. Ibero-Americana, no. 13. Berkeley: University of California Press, 1938.

Spicer, Edward H. "Apuntes sobre el tipo de religión de los Yuto-Aztecas Centrales." *XXXV Congreso Internacional de Mexicanistas. 1962. Actas y Memorias* 2: 27–38. Mexico: Instituto Nacional de Antropología e Historia, 1964.

————. *Cycles of Conquest. The Impact of Spain, Mexico and the United States on the Indians of the Southwest, 1533–1960*. Tucson: University of Arizona Press, 1962.

————. *Perspectives in American Indian Culture Change*. Chicago: University of Chicago Press, 1961.

Stagg, Albert. *The First Bishop of Sonora. Antonio de los Reyes, O.F.M.* Tucson: University of Arizona Press, 1976.

Tamarón y Romeral, Pedro. *Demostración del vastísimo obispado de la Nueva Vizcaya, 1765. Durango, Sinaloa, Arizona, Nuevo México, Chihuahua y porciones de Texas, Coahuila y Zacatecas*. Introduction, bibliography, and annotations by Vito Alessio Robles. Biblioteca Historia Mexicana de Obras Inéditas, no. 7. Mexico: Porrúa, 1937.

Treutlein, Theodore E. "The Economic Regime of the Jesuit Missions in Eighteenth Century Sonora." *Pacific Historical Review* 8 (September 1939): 284–300.

Troncoso, Francisco Paso y. *Las guerras con las tribus Yaqui y Mayo del estado de Sonora*. Mexico: Tip. Dpto. Estado Mayor, 1950.

Villamarín, Juan A. and Judith E. *Indian Labor in Mainland Colonial Spanish America*. Newark, Delaware: University of Delaware Latin American Studies Program Occasional Papers and Monographs, no. 1, 1975.

Villaseñor y Sánchez, D. Joseph Antonio. *Teatro Americano; descripción general de los reynos y provincias de la Nueva España, y sus jurisdicciones*. 2 vols. Mexico: Impr. de la Vda. de D. Joseph Bernardo de Hogal, 1748. Villaseñor was "contador general de la Real Contaduría de Azoques, y cosmógrapho de este reyno."

West, Robert C. *The Mining Community in Northern New Spain: The Parral Mining District*. Ibero-Americana, no. 30. Berkeley: University of California Press, 1949.

Winship, George Parker. "The Coronado Expedition; 1540–42." *14th Annual Report of the Bureau of Ethnology. Part I.* Washington, D.C.: 1896, pp. 339–615.
Includes the original Spanish and an English translation of Pedro Castañeda's *Narrative*.

Wissler, Clark. *The American Indian. An Introduction to the Anthropology of the New World.* 3d ed. New York: Oxford University Press, 1938.

Zambrano, Francisco. *Diccionario Bio-bibliográfico de la Compañía de Jesús en México.* Mexico: Ed. Jus, 1961.
The project, which already comprises ten volumes, is still unfinished.

Acknowledgments

The brevity of these comments is in inverse proportion to the deep gratitude I feel for all who have helped me in my efforts. To the following, please accept my humble thanks:

The directors and staffs of the Archivo General de la Nación de Mexico, Mexico City; the Bancroft Library, University of California, Berkeley, California; Benson Latin American Collection, University of Texas at Austin, The Instituto Nacional de Antropología e Historia, Fondo de Micropelícula, Mexico City; and the Knights of Columbus Vatican Film Library, Pius XII Memorial Library, St. Louis University, St. Louis, Missouri.

To Professors Stanley Ross and Richard Sinkin, of the University of Texas at Austin, directors of my dissertation, to Professor Friedrich Katz of the University of Chicago, mentor and personal inspiration, and to my colleagues in the History Department of Washington University in St. Louis, especially my fellow Latin-Americanist Richard Walter, I want to express my sincere gratitude.

For financial assistance, I wish to thank the Foreign Area Fellowship Program (of the Joint Committee of the Social Science Research Council and the American Council of Learned Scholars) and the Washington University Faculty Summer Research Grant.

Thanks are also due the University of Arizona Press, and especially to Marshall Townsend, Elizabeth Shaw, and Patricia Jones.

Finally, I want to express heartfelt gratitude to my family — my husband Dean, and my daughters Maya and Lauren — for simply being there.

[144]

Index

Indians *(continued)*
  resitance to acculturation
    and assimilation of, 2. *See also*
    Labor; Migration and mobility;
    Pacification; Raids; Rebellions,
    Indian; Tribute and taxation. See
    also *names of individual tribes.*
Inspectors and inspections: royal, 40,
    53, 88–89; Jesuit, 50–52, 89–90;
    by bishop, 92–94
Internal Provinces, 8, 100
Irrigation in Yaqui: natural, 11;
    artificial, 37

Jesuits: arrival in New Spain of,
    22–23; as cultural brokers for In-
    dians, 36; and attack on Huidobro,
    76; and attack on Muni and
    Bernabe, 81–85; and control of
    mission elections, 36,65, 84; and
    control of Indian economy and
    surpluses, 49–50, 84; and corporal
    punishment of Indians, 45; educa-
    tional policies of, for Indians, 36;
    and establishment of Yaqui mis-
    sion, 29–32; evacuation of, from
    northwest, 95–96; expulsion of,
    in 1767, 4–6, 58, 95; and fear of
    Spanish influence on Indians,
    80–81; and fear of *hechiceros,*
    31–32; founding of order of, 22;
    hegemony of, in northwest, 5, 25;
    institutional wealth of, 49, 58; leg-
    acy of, for Yaquis, 3–4; mission
    administration of, 33, 125 n. 39;
    modus operandi of, on frontier,
    23–25; paternalism of, 3–4, 24,
    36–37, 46, 84; and protection of
    Indians, 3; and Yaqui migration to
    mines, 4, 42, 93; and reorganiza-
    tion of Yaqui society, 32–39; and
    supplies for California and Pimería
    missions, 53, 68. *See also* Seculari-
    zation; Trade and commerce; and
    names of individual Jesuits.
Jusacamea, Juan Ignacio (Yaqui). *See*
    Muni and Bernabé
"Just wars," 40

Kino, Eusebio (Jesuit), 52–53

Labor: Indian, for mines, 4–6,
    41–42, 45, 61, 64, 67–68, 74–75;
    Yaqui, for mines, 6, 45, 61, 92, 97,
    102–103; for missionaries, 45,
    67–68, 83–84; payment for,
    83–84; Spanish-Jesuit dispute
    over, 45–48. *See also* Debt
    peonage; *Encomiendas;* Migration
    and mobility; *Repartimientos;*
    Secularization; Slavery
Labor drafts. See *Tapisques*
Land. *See* Yaquis, and communal
    ownership of land; Spaniards, and
    colonization and encroachment on
    Indian land
Land reforms, in the Yaqui, 1–2,
    98–99
Languages: Cáhita, 25, 29, 110 n. 18;
    Nahuatl, 9; Spanish, for Indians,
    36, 102, 113–114 n. 46; Uto-
    Aztecan, 9
Lautaro, Juan, 26–28
Lizasoaín, Ignacio (Jesuit), 89–90
Loyola, Ignatius (Jesuit), 22
Lucenilla family, 72, 120 n. 11,
    124 n. 32
Luque, Francisco de ("Protector of
    Indians"), 45, 47, 49, 83

Macoyahuis, 10
Magistrates, Yaqui, 4, 34–35, 61, 84.
    See also Captains-generals;
    Gobernadores
Maize, 11, 45, 102. *See also*
    Agriculture
Maldonado, Juan Franco, 47–48
Marín, Joseph Francisco, 40
Marquez de Altamira, 85–86
Marquez de Croix (viceroy), 95
Márquina, Diego (Jesuit), 53
Mayo River, 10, 14, 19, 25, 44
Mayos, 3, 10, 14, 19–20, 25–26, 33,
    97; founding of mission of, 29;
    and participation in 1740 Yaqui
    Rebellion, 68, 71, 85; situation of,
    after Jesuit expulsion, 120 n. 82.
    See also Auxiliaries; Censuses
Mazariegos, *Father* (Jesuit), 77
Medicine men. See *Hechiceros*
Mena, Manuel de (lieutenant
    governor), 63–65, 74, 76, 83